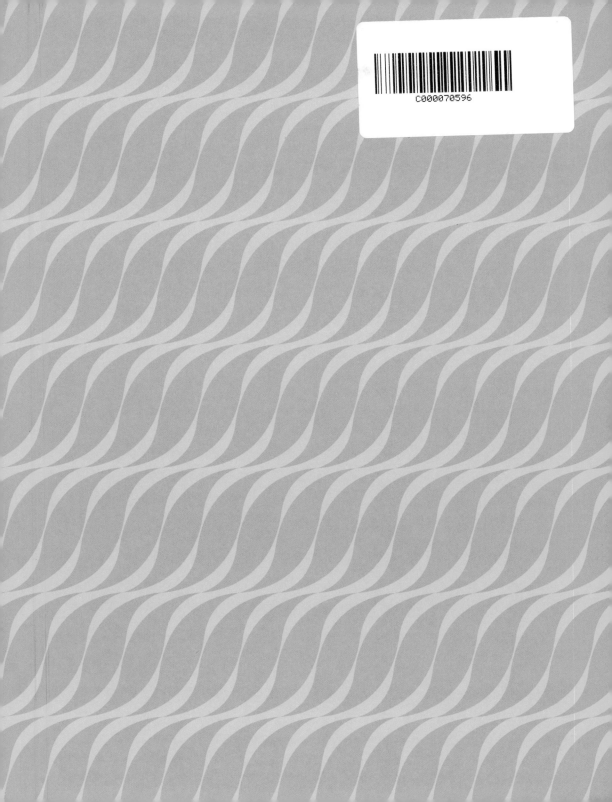

HOW WE LIVED

ART AND ENTERTAINMENT

CULTURE AND RECREATION THROUGH THE AGES

Series Editor Dr John Haywood

southwater

This edition is published by Southwater

Southwater is an imprint of Anness Publishing Ltd
Hermes House, 88–89 Blackfriars Road, London SE1 8HA
tel. 020 7401 2077; fax 020 7633 9499
www.southwaterbooks.com; info@anness.com

© Anness Publishing Ltd 2001, 2003
UK agent: The Manning Partnership Ltd
tel. 01225 478 444; fax 01225 478 440;
sales@manning-partnership.co.uk

UK distributor: Grantham Book Services Ltd
tel. 01476 541080; fax 01476 541061; orders@gbs.tbs-ltd.co.uk

North American agent/distributor: National Book Network
tel. 301 459 3366; fax 301 429 5746; www.nbnbooks.com

Australian agent/distributor: Pan Macmillan Australia
tel. 1300 135 113; fax 1300 135 103; customer.service@macmillan.com.au

A CIP catalogue record for this book is available from the British Library.

Publisher Joanna Lorenz
Managing Editor, Children's Books Gilly Cameron Cooper
Project Editor Rasha Elsaeed
Editorial Reader Jonathan Marshall
"Life, Leisure and Enjoyment" Introduction by Fiona Macdonald
Authors Daud Ali, Jen Green, Charlotte Hurdman, Fiona Macdonald,
Lorna Oakes, Philip Steele, Michael Stotter, Richard Tames
Consultants Nick Allen, Cherry Alexander, Clara Bezanilla, Felicity
Cobbing, Penny Dransart, Jenny Hall, Dr John Haywood, Dr Robin
Holgate, Michael Johnson, Lloyd Laing, Jessie Lim, Heidi Potter, Louise
Schofield, Leslie Webster
Designers Simon Borrough, Matthew Cook, Joyce Mason,
Caroline Reeves, Margaret Sadler, Alison Walker, Stuart Watkinson at Ideas
Into Print, Sarah Williams
Special Photography John Freeman
Stylists Konika Shakar, Thomasina Smith, Melanie Williams

PICTURE CREDITS
b=bottom, t=top, c=centre, l=left, r=right
Leslie and Roy Adkins Picture Library: 30l, 31br; AKG: 12cr, 13cr, 13tr &
13cl, 47c, 49tl, 51tl; B and C Alexander: 9tr, 18tl & 18c, 19tl, 19cl & 19tr;
The Ancient Art and Architecture Collections Ltd: 7r, 10r, 11r, 14tl & 14cl,
15c, 24t, 25cl & 25br, 36tr, 37tcr, 39cl, 54t, 55t; Charles Tait/AAA
Collection: 59bl; Corbis-Bettmann: 43tl, 43cl & 43br; The Bridgeman Art
Library Ltd: 9c, 12tl & 12cl, 14tr, Standing Courtesan by Kaigetsudo 16br,
Collecting Insects by Harunobu 17tl, 27bl, 33l & 33r, Courtesan with Musical
Instrument by Kuniyoshi 4tl, 48tl, Urban Life 49tr, 51c; The following
Bridgeman Art Library images are reproduced by kind permission of the
Fitzwilliam Museum Cambridge: Celebrated Beauties by Utamaro 16tl;
The British Museum: 11l, 39tl; Bulloz: 52tl; Rennes Cedex: 44tl; Christies
Images: 3tl, 17tr; Bruce Coleman: 8tp; Corbis: 6tl; C M Dixon: Cover c, 8c,
25tr, 30br, 37cl, 38tl, 39tr, 40t, 41tl, 41cl & 41bl, 42tr, 43tr & 43bl, 55b; E T
Archive: 23c, 26br, 28tl, 29tr & 29bl, 46cl, 57cl, 61tl; Mary Evans Picture
Library: 40b; Werner Forman Archive: 20cl, 21tr, 26bl, 32l & 32r, 49bc, 56c
& 56tr, 58bl; Sonia Halliday Photographs: 30tr; Historic Scotland: 45tl;
Michael Holford: 20tr, 36cl, 37tr, 41br; The Hutchinson Library: 34cl;
The Idemitsu Museum of Art: 2b, 17cl; Japan Archive: 48br; Peter Newark's
Pictures: 43bl; NHPA: 8cl; MacQuitty Collections: 27bl, 35tl, 35tr & 35cl,
56tr; Murial and Giovanni Dagli Orti: 22t, 52cr; Radiotimes Hulton
Picture Library: 54b; Stuart Rae: 59tr; Sacamoto Photo Research
Laboratory/ Corbis: 17bl; Scotland in Focus: 59tl; Mick Sharp: 58tl;
South American Photo Library: 47tl & 47c, 60c; V & A Picture Library:
59tl & 59cl; Visual Arts Library: 1, 5tl, 5tl, 26t, 27tl & 27tr, 28tl & 28c,
30tr, 57tl, 60tl & 60tr; ZEFA: 10l

Previously published as *Art, Culture & Entertainment*

10 9 8 7 6 5 4 3 2 1

CONTENTS

THE WRITTEN TRADITION

KEY
Look out for the patterns used throughout this book, there is one for each culture

The Stone Age	Japan	North American
Mesopotamia	Ancient Greece	Indians
Ancient Egypt	Roman Empire	The Arctic
India	The Celts	Aztec & Maya
China	The Vikings	Inca Empire

Life, Leisure, and Enjoyment

Daily life is more than just working, eating, and sleeping. From the time of the earliest organized human societies, more than 50,000 years ago, men and women have enjoyed telling stories, listening to music, dancing, and playing games. Early humans decorated their clothes, tools, weapons, and shelters with patterns and magic symbols. They even created lifelike images of the world around them. The earliest-known paintings of people and animals—discovered in caves in Europe—date from almost 30,000 years ago. The artwork is skilled, which suggests a long tradition of artists working for hundreds of years before, slowly perfecting their techniques. It seems clear that, even though early peoples' lives were often a struggle for survival in a harsh environment, there was time to draw and paint.

Animals were often depicted in cave paintings. They are believed to represent the creatures that Stone Age people hunted for food.

Music has always been a popular form of entertainment in Japan. This woman is playing a *shamisen*—a three-stringed instrument.

Sculpture, ornaments, and painting have always been important for many reasons. Most simply, people like things to look

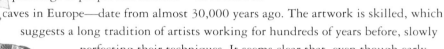

Timeline 50,000 b.c.–500 b.c.

*c.*50,000 b.c. The first evidence of body decoration. Dead people are buried wearing shells and red ocher.

*c.*23,000 b.c. Small statues of plump women, called "Venus figurines" are made in Europe.

Early humans made jewelry from shells

*c.*15,000 b.c. Some of the finest cave paintings are made in Europe.

*c.*3000 b.c. The first written script, called *cuneiform* (wedge-shaped), develops in Mesopotamia.

*c.*3100 b.c. The Egyptians use hieroglyphs (picture-symbols) for writing.

*c.*3,000 b.c. The start of Chinese pottery-making.

Ancient Egyptian hieroglyphs

*c.*2500 b.c. The earliest surviving evidence of Indian jewelry (bangles and ear-studs) and makeup tools.

*c.*1550–1070 b.c. The New Kingdom

50,000 b.c.   15,000 b.c.   2500 b.c.   1500 b

good. All around the world, craftworkers made everyday

Tribal peoples valued the skills that went into creating patterned pots.

items, such as blankets or food baskets, as attractive as possible. The type and style of decoration used varied from culture to culture, and over the centuries. The available materials were also important, such as clay for pottery, or colored pigments for paints and dyes. Wealthy people could afford items made from valuable substances, such as silk or porcelain (both from China), or employ skilled artists to create fine statues, carvings, pottery, and mosaics, such as those surviving from ancient Greece and Rome.

People have also always liked to look good. Men and women in ancient Egypt wore makeup and had elaborate hairstyles. In India, traditional clothing was simple, but people wore fancy accessories and jewels. In many civilizations, people have also liked decorating their own bodies, with piercing, body paint, and tattoos.

An Aztec woman is shown wearing bangles, a chunky necklace, and earrings. She obviously took a lot of pride in her appearance.

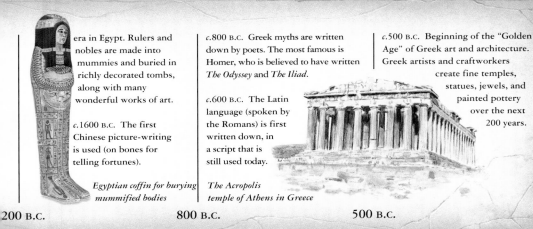

era in Egypt. Rulers and nobles are made into mummies and buried in richly decorated tombs, along with many wonderful works of art.

*c.*1600 B.C. The first Chinese picture-writing is used (on bones for telling fortunes).

Egyptian coffin for burying mummified bodies

*c.*800 B.C. Greek myths are written down by poets. The most famous is Homer, who is believed to have written *The Odyssey* and *The Iliad*.

*c.*600 B.C. The Latin language (spoken by the Romans) is first written down, in a script that is still used today.

The Acropolis temple of Athens in Greece

*c.*500 B.C. Beginning of the "Golden Age" of Greek art and architecture. Greek artists and craftworkers create fine temples, statues, jewels, and painted pottery over the next 200 years.

200 B.C.   800 B.C.   500 B.C.

Patterns, pictures, stories, myths, legends, dancing, and music added an extra layer of meaning to people's lives. They helped people to express their beliefs, manage their fears and sometimes (they thought), to make contact with the invisible world of gods, spirits, ghosts, and dead ancestors. Some art forms offered magical protection to hunters and children. Others, such as costumes and jewelry were used in ceremonies that marked important stages in people's lives, such as birth, marriage, or death.

The arts often provided excellent entertainment. Watching skilled performances—from simple tunes played on prehistoric deer-bone flutes to elegant Japanese court theater—gave people pleasure. Sometimes, they helped them to understand their feelings, hopes and fears, and the world around them. Singers, poets, and storytellers retold ancient myths in words and music. This often became a way of preserving the history of families and tribes. Around 5,000 years ago,

Chinese letters are called characters. They are read down, from right to left.

The decorations of North American Indian tribes, such as this rattle, often had spiritual significance.

This Mesopotamian board game may have been played like Ludo. It is made from wood and decorated with a mosaic of shell and colored stone.

Timeline 400 B.C.–A.D. 1700

380 B.C. Servian Wall is built to defend Rome from attack. Over the next 500 years, Roman architects and engineers designed and built many roads, forts, water systems, and fine public buildings (such as temples and amphitheaters) in the lands ruled by Rome.

292 B.C. The Maya people of Central

Chinese calligraphy

America begin to write using picture symbols.

A.D. 300–700 The Moche people of South America are expert goldsmiths.

A.D. 868 First printed book produced using woodblocks, in China.

A.D. 750–1100 The Viking age. The Vikings are expert metalworkers, and they also enjoy music and sagas (dramatic adventure stories).

A.D. 1040 Chinese invent new form of printing using moveable type.

1300 Start of Noh drama in Japan. Plays performed by male actors only.

1300–1500 Chancay and Inca peoples of Peru create brilliantly colored clothes decorated with beads and

400 B.C.	A.D. 300	A.D. 800	1300

Ancient civilizations in the Near East, such as those of Egypt and Mesopotamia, put great effort into creating visually stunning interiors. This is the internal hall of a Mesopotamian palace.

in the Middle East, artists and craftworkers also began to use picture symbols to record useful information or important events. Picture-writing was also developed in China before 1500 B.C. From that time on, many people around the world used writing as a new art form. It was another way of passing on traditions, telling ancient stories, myths, and legends, or expressing important beliefs and ideas.

In a thematic history such as this, you can follow developments in different aspects of art and culture in turn. You will be able to see how dress, accessories, sport, entertainmnent, ornamental and decorative arts, writing and storytelling evolved through time and varied from culture to culture.

Greek girls were expected to spend their time helping in the home, but many still had time to enjoy a game of tag.

Costumes at the Inca August Festival

feathers, many of which they wear to seasonal festivals.

1500 A new garment, a long, loose robe called a *kimono,* becomes fashionable in Japan.

1500s to 1700s Musicians and dancers entertain Mughal rulers at royal courts in India. The Mughals also collect beautiful books, paintings, and jewels.

1600 Start of Japanese Kabuki popular drama and bunraku puppet plays.

Kabuki actor

1500   1600   1700

Stone Age Jewelry

CEREMONIAL DRESS
The amazing headdress, face painting and jewelry still seen at ceremonies in Papua New Guinea may echo the richness of decoration in Stone Age times.

M EN AND WOMEN WORE JEWELLERY from as early as the Stone Age. Necklaces and pendants were made from all sorts of natural objects. Brightly colored pebbles, snail shells, fish bones, animal teeth, seashells, eggshells, nuts, and seeds were all used. Later, semi-precious amber and jade, fossilized jet, and handmade clay beads were also used. The beads were threaded onto thin strips of leather or twine made from plant fibers.

Other jewelry included bracelets made of slices of elephant or mammoth tusk. Strings of shells and teeth were made into beautiful headbands. Women braided their hair and put it up with combs and pins. People probably decorated their bodies and outlined their eyes with pigments such as red ocher. They may have tattooed and pierced their bodies too.

BODY PAINT
These Australian Aboriginal children have painted their bodies with clay. They have used patterns that are thousands of years old.

BONES AND TEETH
Necklaces were often made from the bones and teeth of a walrus. This one comes from Skara Brae in the Orkney Islands, Scotland. A hole was made in each bead with a stone tool, or with a wooden stick spun by a bow drill. The beads were then strung onto a strip of leather or twine.

MAKE A NECKLACE
You will need: self-drying clay, rolling pin and board, modeling tool, sandpaper, ivory and black acrylic paint, paintbrush, water, ruler, scissors, chamois leather, cardboard, double-sided tape, white glue, leather laces.

1 Roll out the clay on a board and cut out four crescent shapes with the modeling tool. Leave them on the board to dry.

2 Rub the crescents lightly with sandpaper and paint them an ivory color. You could varnish them later to make them shiny.

3 Cut four strips of leather about 3½ x 1¼ in. Use the edge of a piece of cardboard to make a black criss-cross pattern on the strips.

NATURAL DECORATION

We know about the wide variety of materials used in Stone Age jewelry from cave paintings and ornaments discovered in graves. Shells were highly prized and some were traded over long distances. Other materials included deers' teeth, mammoth and walrus ivory, fish bones, and birds' feathers.

a selection of sea shells

A WARRIOR'S HEADDRESS

The headdress of this Yali warrior from Indonesia is made of wild boars' teeth. The necklace is made of shells and bone. Headdresses and necklaces made of animals' teeth may have had a spiritual meaning for Stone Age people. The wearer may have believed that the teeth brought the strength or courage of the animal from which they came.

BANGLES AND EAR STUDS

Jewelry found at Harappa in Pakistan included these items. They date from between 2300 B.C. and 1750 B.C. and are made from shells and colored pottery. Archaeologists in Harappa have found remains of the shops that sold jewelry.

Stone Age people believed that wearing a leopard claw necklace brought them magical powers.

4 When they are dry, fold back the edges of each strip and hold in place with double-sided tape.

5 Brush the middle of each crescent with glue and wrap the leather around, forming a loop at the top, as shown.

6 Braid together three leather laces to make a thong. Make the thong long enough to go around your neck and be tied.

7 Thread the leopard's claws onto the middle of the thong, arranging them so that there are small spaces between them.

Egyptian Vanity

THE ANCIENT EGYPTIANS were very fond of jewelry. The rich wore pieces finely crafted from precious stones and metals. Cheaper adornments were made from glass and polished stones. Makeup was also important for both men and women. They wore green eyeshadow made from a mineral called malachite and black eyeliner made from galena, a type of lead. Lipsticks and blusher were made from red ocher. The Egyptians liked to tattoo their skin, and they also used perfumes. Most men were clean shaven. Wigs were worn by men and women, even by those who had plenty of hair of their own. Gray hair was dyed and there were various remedies for baldness.

A TIMELESS BEAUTY
This limestone head is of Queen Nefertiti, the wife of the Sun-worshipping pharaoh Akhenaten. She seems to be the ideal of Egyptian beauty. She wears a headdress and a necklace. The stone is painted and so we can see that she is also wearing makeup and lipstick.

LOOKING GOOD
Mirrors were made of polished copper or bronze, with handles of wood or ivory. This bronze mirror is from 1900 B.C. Mirrors were used by the wealthy for checking hairstyles, applying makeup, or simply for admiring their own good looks! The poor had to make do with seeing their reflection in water.

MAKE A MIRROR
You will need: mirror card, pencil, scissors, self-drying clay, modeling tool, rolling pin and board, small piece of cardboard or sandpaper, gold paint, glue and brush, water pot and

1 Begin by drawing a mirror shape on the white side of a piece of mirror card, as shown. Carefully cut the mirror shape out. Put the card to one side.

2 Take your clay and roll it into a tube. Then mold it into a handle shape, as shown. Decorate the handle with a lotus or papyrus flower, or other design.

3 Now make a slot in the handle with a square piece of card or sandpaper, as shown. This is where the mirror card will slot into the handle.

BIG WIGS AND WAXY CONES

Many pictures show nobles at banquets wearing cones of perfumed grease on their heads. The scent may have been released as the cones melted in the heat. However, some experts believe that the cones were drawn in by artists to show that the person was wearing a scented wig. False hairpieces and wigs were very popular in Egypt. It was common for people to cut their hair short, but some did have long hair that they dressed in elaborate styles.

COSMETICS

During the early years of the Egyptian Empire, black-eye kohl was made from galena, a type of poisonous lead! Later, soot was used. Henna was painted on the nails and the soles of the feet to make them red. Popular beauty treatments included pumice stone to smooth rough skin and ash face packs.

face pack   *pumice stone*   *kohl*   *henna*

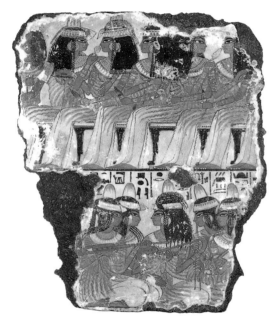

COSMETICS BOWL

Makeup, oils, and lotions were prepared and stored in jars and bowls, as well as in hollow reeds or tubes. These containers were made of stone, pottery, and glass. Minerals were ground into a powder and then mixed with water in cosmetics bowls to make a paste. Makeup was applied with the fingers or with a special wooden applicator. Two colors of eye makeup were commonly used—green and black. Green was used in the early period, but later the distinctive black eye paint became more popular.

The shape of mirrors and their shining surface reminded Egyptians of the Sun disk, so they became religious symbols. By the New Kingdom, many were decorated with the goddess Hathor or lotus flowers.

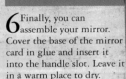

4 Place the handle on a wire baking tray and leave it in a warm place to dry. Turn it over after two hours. When it is completely dry, try your mirror for size.

5 It is now time to paint the handle. Paint one side carefully with gold paint and let it dry. When it has dried, turn the handle over and paint the other side.

6 Finally, you can assemble your mirror. Cover the base of the mirror card in glue and insert it into the handle slot. Leave it in a warm place to dry.

EGYPTIAN VANITY   11

Clothing and Jewelry in India

BOTH RICH AND POOR PEOPLE IN INDIA have always tended to wear simple clothes dressed up with lots of jewelry, such as earrings, armbands, breastplates, nose rings, and anklets. They also had elaborate hairstyles decorated with flowers and ornaments.

Religious beliefs influenced how people dressed. Hindu men and women dressed simply in a single piece of fabric that was draped around the hips, drawn up between the legs, then fastened securely again at the waist. For men this was called a *dhoti*. Women wore bodices above the waist but men were often barechested. The female style of dress evolved into the *sari*.

When Islam arrived in India, tailored garments became widespread in the north of the country. People wore sewn cotton pants called *paijama* or *shalwar*, with a long tunic called a *kamiz* or *kurta*. For men, turbans became popular. Muslim women were expected to dress modestly, so they began to wear veils, a practice that Hindu women also adopted.

SETTING THE TREND
Bangles and ear studs from the Indus Valley are among the earliest ornaments found in India. They are more than 4,000 years old. The styles of these pieces of jewelry, and the designs on them, were used again in later forms of decoration.

BEAUTY AIDS
This mirror, collyrium applicator, and hair pin are more than 4,000 years old. Large dark eyes were considered a sign of beauty, so women drew attention to their eyes by outlining them with collyrium, a black substance.

ANCIENT DRESS
A painted fragment of a pillar shows a woman wearing a long red skirt and jewelry. The pillar is about 2,000 years old.

MAKE A FLOWER BRACELET

You will need: 8½ x 6 in. sheets of thin white cardboard, pencil, scissors, gold paint, paintbrush, sheets of white paper, white glue, foil sweet papers, gardening wire, pliers.

1 Draw some simple flower shapes on the white card. They should be about ¾ in. in diameter. Give each flower six rounded petals.

2 Carefully cut out each of the flower shapes. Then paint both sides of each flower with gold paint. Let the flowers dry thoroughly.

3 Draw 10 to 12 wedge shapes on the white paper sheets. They should be wider at the bottom than at the top. Cut out the wedge shapes.

COLORFUL SILK

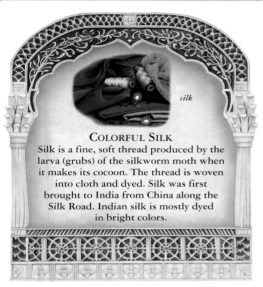

Silk is a fine, soft thread produced by the larva (grubs) of the silkworm moth when it makes its cocoon. The thread is woven into cloth and dyed. Silk was first brought to India from China along the Silk Road. Indian silk is mostly dyed in bright colors.

silk

HINDU DRESS

In this detail from a painted panel, a Hindu man and woman wear typical dress— a *dhoti* for the man and for the woman, a *sari*. Both men and women liked to wear brightly colored clothes.

JEWELS FOR ALL

A Rajasthani woman wears traditional jewelry and dress. Nowadays in India, jewelry is still so valued that even the poorer peasants own pieces for special occasions.

Floral designs are common patterns used throughout Indian art.

CLOTHING FOR THE COURT

Courtiers from the Mughal Empire (1526–1857) wore a side-fastening coat called a *jama*. It has a tight body, high waist, and flared skirt reaching to below the knees. It is worn over tight-fitting pants, or *paijama*, gathered at the ankle. A sash, called a *patuka*, is tied to the waist. Courtiers also wore a small turban as a mark of respect.

4 Apply glue to the wedge shapes and roll them up to make beads, leaving a hole through the middle. Paint the beads gold and let dry.

5 Carefully cut out tiny circles from the colored foil paper. Make sure you have enough to stick onto the center of each flower.

6 Measure gardening wire long enough to go around your wrist. Add 1½ in. for a loop. Tape the flowers to the wire and thread on the beads.

7 To finish the flower bracelet, use a pair of pliers to bend back one end of the wire to form a loop and the other end to form a hook.

Greek Garments

PHYSICAL BEAUTY AND AN ATTRACTIVE appearance were admired in ancient Greece in both men and women. Clothes were simple and practical, and made of wool and linen, which were spun at home. The rich, however, could afford more luxurious garments made from imported cotton or silk. Fabrics were colored with dyes made from plants, insects, and shellfish.

Men and women wore long tunics, draped loosely for comfort in the warm climate, and held in place with decorative pins or brooches. A heavy cloak was added for traveling or in bad weather. The tunics of soldiers and laborers were cut short, so they could move easily. Sandals were usually worn outdoors, though men sometimes wore boots. In hot weather, hats made of straw or wool kept off the sun. A tan was not admired in ancient Greece, because it signified outdoor work as a laborer or a slave. Men cut their hair short, while women coiled long hair in elaborate styles, sometimes with ribbons.

SEE FOR YOURSELF
Glass mirrors were not known to the Greeks. Instead, they used highly polished bronze to see their reflection in. This mirror has a handle in the shaped of a woman. Winged sphinxes sit on her shoulders.

GOLDEN LION
This heavy bracelet dates from around the 4th century B.C. It is made of solid gold and decorated with two lion heads. Gold was valuable because there was little of it found in Greece. Most of it was imported from Asia Minor or Egypt.

KEEP IT SIMPLE
The figurine above is wearing a peplos. This was a simple, sleeveless dress worn by Greek women. The only adornment was a belt tied underneath the bust. This statue comes from a Greek colony in southern Italy.

CHITON
You will need: tape measure, rectangle of cloth, scissors, pins, chalk, needle, thread, 12 metal buttons (with loops), cord.

1 Ask a friend to measure your width from wrist to wrist, double this figure. Measure your length from shoulder to ankle. Cut your cloth to these figures.

2 Fold the fabric in half widthwise. Pin the two sides together. Draw a chalk line along the fabric, ¾ in. away from the edge of the fabric.

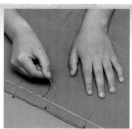

3 Sew along the chalk line. Then turn the material inside out, so the seam is on the inside. Refold the fabric so the seam is at the back.

TEXTILE TRADE

Clothes in ancient Greece were usually made from wool and linen. The Greeks exported their wool, which was admired for its superior quality. Cotton and silk were imported to make clothes. But only wealthy Greeks could afford clothes made from these materials.

cotton

linen

raw wool

POWDER POT

Greek women used face powder and other cosmetics and kept them in a ceramic pot called a pyxis. This one was was made in Athens in about 450 B.C. The painted decoration shows women spinning and weaving.

Clothes were handmade in ancient Greece. Enough material would be woven to fit the person they were being made for exactly, to avoid waste.

spiral band

BURIAL JEWELRY

Some pieces of jewelry, like the ones pictured here, were made especially for burial. Very thin sheet gold was beaten into belts and wreaths. Important people like the Kings and Queens of Macedonia were buried in crowns of gold leaves.

wreath

belt

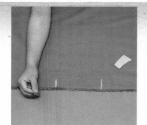

4 Make a gap big enough for your head to fit in, at one of the open ends of the fabric. Mark where the gap is going to be and pin the fabric together there.

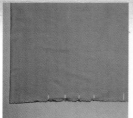

5 From the head gap mark a point every 2 in. to the end of the fabric. Pin together the front and back along these points. Your arms will fit through here.

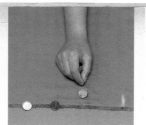

6 At each pin, sew on a button to hold the two sides of material together. To secure the button, sew through the loop several times and knot it.

7 Cut a length of cord, to fit around your waist with a little bit spare to tie. Tie this cord around your waist and bunch the material up, over the cord.

Palace Fashions in Japan

CLOTHING IN EARLY TIMES often depended on how rich you were. In Japan, from around A.D. 600 to 1500, wealthy noble men and women at the emperor's court wore very different clothes from ordinary peasant farmers. Fashions were based on traditional Chinese styles. Both men and women wore long, flowing robes made of many layers of fine, glossy silk, held in place by a sash and cords. Men also wore wide pants underneath. Women kept their hair loose and long, while men tied their hair into a topknot and wore a tall black hat. Elegance and refinement were the aims of this style.

After about 1500, wealthy samurai families began to wear *kimono*—long, loose robes. *Kimono* also became popular among wealthy artists, actors, and craftworkers. The shoguns passed laws to try to stop ordinary people from wearing elaborate *kimono*, but they proved impossible to enforce.

PARASOL
Women protected their delicate complexions with sunshades made of oiled paper. The fashion was for pale skin, often heavily powdered, with dark, soft eyebrows.

GOOD TASTE OR GAUDY?
This woman's outfit dates from the 1700s. Though striking, it would probably have been considered too bold to be in the most refined taste. Men and women took great care in choosing garments that blended well together.

MAKE A FAN
You will need: thick cardboard (15 x 10¼ in.), pencil, ruler, compasses, protractor, felt tip pen (blue), paper (red), scissors, paints, paintbrush, water pot, glue stick.

1 Draw a line down the center of the piece of cardboard. Place your compasses two-thirds of the way up the line. Draw a circle 9 in. in diameter.

2 Add squared-off edges at the top of the circle, as shown. Now draw your handle (6 in. long). The handle should be directly over the vertical line.

3 Place a protractor at the top of the handle and draw a semicircle around it. Now mark lines every 2.5 degrees. Draw pencil lines through these marks.

FEET OFF THE GROUND

To catch insects in a garden by lamplight these women are wearing *geta* (clogs). *Geta* were designed to protect the wearer's feet from mud and rain by raising them about 2–3 inches above the ground. They were worn outdoors.

SILK *KIMONO*

This beautiful silk *kimono* was made in about 1600. Women wore a wide silk sash called an *obi* on top of their *kimono*. Men fastened their *kimono* with a narrow sash.

PAPER FAN

Folding fans, made of pleated paper, were a Japanese invention. They were carried by both men and women. This one is painted with gold leaf and chrysanthemum flowers.

BEAUTIFUL HAIR

Traditional palace fashions for men and women are shown in this scene from the imperial palace. The women have long, flowing hair that reaches to their waists—a sign of great beauty in early Japan.

It was the custom for Japanese noblewomen to hide their faces in court. They used decorated fans such as this one as a screen. Fans were also used to help people keep cool on hot, humid summer days.

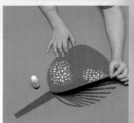

4 Draw a blue line ½ in. to the left of each line you have drawn. Then draw a blue line ⅛ in. to the right of this line. Add a squiggle between sections.

5 Cut out your cardboard fan. Now use this as a template. Draw around the fan top (not handle) onto your red paper. Cut out the red paper.

6 Now cut out the in-between sections on your cardboard fan (those marked with a squiggle). Paint the fan brown on both sides. Let dry.

7 Paint the red paper with white flowers. Let it dry. Paste glue onto one side of the cardboard fan. Stick the undecorated side of the red paper to the fan.

Cold-climate Dress

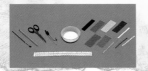

In the freezing Arctic, clothes needed to be warm as well as beautiful. Strips or patches of different furs were used to form designs and geometric patterns on outer clothes. Fur trimmings, toggles, and other decorative fastenings added the final touches to many clothes. Jewelry included pendants, bracelets, necklaces, and brooches. These ornaments were traditionally made of natural materials, such as bone and walrus ivory.

In North America, Inuit women often decorated clothes with birds' beaks, tiny feathers or even porcupine quills. In Greenland, lace and glass beads were popular decorations. Saami clothes were the most colorful in the Arctic. Saami men, women, and children wore blue outfits with a bright red and yellow trim. Men's costumes included a tall hat and a short flared tunic. Women's clothes included flared skirts with embroidered hems and colorful hats, shawls, and scarves.

Saami Costume

A Saami man wears the traditional costume of his region, including a flared tunic trimmed with bright woven ribbon at the neck, shoulders, cuffs, and hem. Outfits such as the one above were worn year-round. In winter, Saami people wore thick fur parkas, called *peskes,* over the bright tunics.

Bear Toggle

An ivory toggle carved into the shape of a polar bear completes this traditional sealskin jacket. Arctic people took great pride in their appearance and loved to decorate their clothes in this way. In ancient times, the Inuit, for example, decorated their garments with hundreds of tiny feathers or the claws of mammals, such as foxes or hares. Women often decorated all the family's clothes.

Make a Saami Hat

You will need: red felt (22¼ x 11¼ in.), white glue, glue brush, black ribbon (22¼ x ¼ in.), colored ribbon, white felt, ruler, pencil, compass, red card, scissors, red, green and white ribbon (3 at 17¼ x 1¼ in.), red ribbon

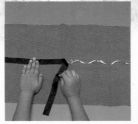

1 Mark out the center of the red felt along its length. Carefully glue the length of black ribbon along the center line, as shown above.

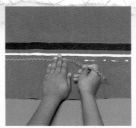

2 Continue to decorate the felt with different kinds of colored ribbon and white felt, making a series of strips along the red felt, as shown above.

3 Cut out a circle of red cardboard with a diameter of 7 in. Draw a circle inside with a diameter of 6 in. Cut into the larger circle to the 6 in. line.

CURVING BOOT

This picture shows a curved boot worn by the Saami people from Arctic Scandinavia. These boots are designed for use with skis and are decorated with traditional woolen pompoms. The curved boot tips stop the skier from slipping out of the skis when traveling uphill.

WEDDING FINERY

The bride, bridegroom, and a guest at a Saami wedding in north Norway all wear the traditional outfits. Notice that the style of the man's wedding hat differs from the one shown in the picture on the opposite page. Both men and women wear brooches encrusted with metal discs. Saami women's wedding outfits include tall hats, tasseled shawls, and ribbons.

BEADS AND LACE

A woman from western Greenland wears the traditional beaded costume of her nation, which includes a top with a wide black collar and cuffs, and high sealskin boots. After European settlers arrived in Greenland, glass beads, and lace became traditional decorations on clothing. Hundreds of beads were sewn onto jackets to make intricate patterns.

The style of Saami hats varied from region to region. In southern Norway, men's hats were tall and rounded. Further north, their hats had four points.

4 Glue the ends of the decorated red felt together, as shown above. You will need to find the right size to fit around your head.

5 Fold down the tabs cut into the red cardboard circle. Glue the tabs, then stick the cardboard circle to the felt inside one end of the hat.

6 While the hat is drying, glue the colored ribbon strips together. Glue these strips 6 in. from the end of the 22¾ in. long red ribbon band.

7 Glue the 22¾ in. band of red ribbon onto the base of the hat, making sure the shorter strips of red, green, and white ribbons go over the top of the band.

Bold Designs in South America

Festival costumes in the Andes today are in dazzling pinks, reds, and blues. In the Inca period it was no different. People loved to wear brightly colored braids, threads, and ribbons. Sequins, beads, feathers, and gold were sewn into fabric, while precious stones, red shells, silver, and gold were made into beautiful earplugs, necklaces, pendants, nose rings, and disks. However, it was only the nobles who were allowed to show off by wearing feathers, jewels, and precious metals. Some of the most prized ornaments were gifts from the emperor for high-ranking service in the army.

Much of the finest craft work went into making small statues and objects for religious ceremonies, temples, and shrines. During the Inca period, craft workers were employed by the State. They produced many beautiful treasures, but some of the best of these were the work of non-Inca peoples, particularly the Chimú. Treasures shipped to Spain after the Conquest astounded the Europeans by their fine craftsmanship.

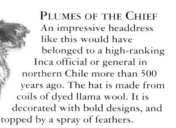

PLUMES OF THE CHIEF
An impressive headdress like this would have belonged to a high-ranking Inca official or general in northern Chile more than 500 years ago. The hat is made from coils of dyed llama wool. It is decorated with bold designs, and topped by a spray of feathers.

A SACRED PUMA
This gold pouch in the shape of a puma, a sacred animal, was made by the Moche people between 1,300 and 1,700 years ago. It may have been used to carry *coca* leaves. These were used as a drug during religious ceremonies. The pattern on the body is made up of two-headed snakes.

A GOLD AND SILVER NECKLACE
You will need: self-drying clay, cutting board, ruler, large blunt needle, gold and silver paint, paintbrush, water pot, cardboard, pencil, scissors, strong thread.

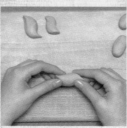

1 Form pieces of clay into beads in the shape of peanuts. You will need 10 large beads (about 1½ x ¾ in.) and 10 smaller beads (about 1 x ½ in.).

2 Use the needle to mark patterns on the beads, so that they look like nut shells. Then carefully make a hole through the middle of each bead. Let dry.

3 Paint half the shells of each size gold and half of them silver. You should have 5 small and 5 large gold beads, and 5 small and 5 large silver beads.

PRECIOUS AND PRETTY

The most valued stone in the Andes was blue-green turquoise. It was cut and polished into beads and disks for necklaces, and inlaid in gold statues and masks. Blue lapis lazuli, black jet, and other stones also found their way along trading routes. Colombia, on the northern edge of the Inca Empire, mined many precious stones and metals. Seashells were cut and polished into beautiful beads.

emerald   *turquoise*

lapis lazuli

BIRDS OF A FEATHER

Birds and fish decorate this feather cape. It was made by the Chancay people of the central Peruvian coast between the 1300s and 1500s. It would have been worn for religious ceremonies. Feather work was a skilled craft in both Central and South America. In Inca times, the brilliantly colored feathers of birds called macaws were sent to the emperor as tribute from the tribes of the Amazon forests.

Necklaces made of gold, silver, and jewels would only have been worn by Inca royalty, such as the Quya *(Inca empress).*

TREASURE LOST AND FOUND

A beautifully made gold pendant created in the Moche period before the Incas rose to power. After the Spanish conquest of Peru, countless treasures were looted from temples or palaces by Spanish soldiers. Gold was melted down or shipped back to Europe. A few items escaped by being buried in graves. Some have been discovered by archaeologists.

4 Paint some cardboard gold on both sides. On it draw 11 rectangles (1¼ x ½ in.) with rounded ends. Cut them out and carefully prick a hole in each end.

5 Thread the needle and make a knot 4 in. from the end of the thread. Then thread the cardboard strips and large beads alternately, using the gold beads first.

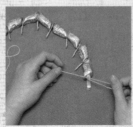

6 Be sure to start and end with card strips. When you have finished, knot the thread next to the last card strip. Cut the thread 4 in. from the knot.

7 Repeat steps 5 and 6 using more thread and the small beads, so that the beads are joined as shown. Finally, knot the ends of the two threads together.

Interior Design in Assyria

WOMAN IN A WINDOW
A piece of carved ivory from Phoenicia. The Phoenicians probably supplied the Assyrians with most of their ivory. They were great traders from the eastern Mediterranean shores.

ASSYRIAN KINGS IN NORTH MESOPOTAMIA (present-day Iraq) loved the luxury of ivory furniture. They filled their palaces with ivory beds, arm chairs, foot stools, and tables. No complete pieces of ivory furniture have survived to modern times, but archaeologists found part of an ivory throne during their excavations at the city of Nimrud in the 1840s. They also found some elephant tusks and many small, carved ivory plaques that were once attached to the wooden framework of pieces of furniture. Today, it is considered cruel to kill elephants for their ivory, and the animals have become an endangered species.

No textiles have survived but Assyrian palaces would probably have been made comfortable with cushions and woolen rugs. Stone entrances to the palace rooms carved in the form of floral-patterned carpets give us an idea of what the rugs may have looked like.

INSIDE THE PALACE
Palaces were built from mud brick, but the lower interior walls were decorated with carved and painted slabs of stone. Teams of sculptors and artists produced scenes showing the king's military campaigns and wild bull and lion hunts. The upper walls were plastered and painted with similar scenes to glorify the king and impress foreign visitors. Paints were ground from minerals. Red and brown paints were made from ochers, blues, and greens from copper ores, azurite, and malachite.

MAKE A BRONZE AND IVORY MIRROR

You will need: pencil, strong white and reflective (silver) card stock, ruler, scissors, thick dowel, water, flour and newspaper to make papier mâché, masking tape, paints, brushes, sandpaper, glue.

1 Draw around a saucer to mark a circle 4¾ in. across onto the white card stock. Add a handle about 2½ in. long and 1 in. wide as shown. Cut out.

2 Take a length of dowel measuring about 8 in. long. Fix the dowel to the handle using masking tape. Bend the card stock around the dowel as shown.

3 Scrunch up a piece of newspaper into a ball. Attach the newspaper ball to the top of the handle with masking tape as shown.

LUXURY IN THE GARDEN

King Ashurbanipal and his wife even had luxurious ivory furniture in the palace gardens at Nineveh. In this picture, the king is reclining on an elaborate ivory couch decorated with tiny carved and gilded lions. The queen is sitting on an ivory chair with a high back and resting her feet on a foot stool. Cushions make the furniture more comfortable. Ivory workers used drills and chisels similar to those used by carpenters. The ivory plaques had signs on them to show how they should be fitted together.

SOURCES OF IVORY

Ivory furniture came from Phoenicia as booty. The Phoenicians had two main sources of elephant ivory. From the 15th to the 9th centuries B.C . there were elephants in nearby Syria, although they do not live there today. This would have been their nearest source. The Phoenicians were great sailors and often went to Egypt where they may well have traded some of their goods for ivory that had come from Africa.

ivory

African elephant

Polished bronze was used for mirrors in ancient times. A mirror with a handle of carved ivory like this would have belonged to a wealthy woman.

BOY-EATER

This furniture plaque shows a boy being eaten by a lioness. Sometimes ivory was stained or inlaid with paste to imitate jewels. The boy's kilt is covered with gold leaf, and his curly hair is made of tiny gold pins. There are lotus flowers and papyrus plants in the background, inlaid with real lapis lazuli and carnelian.

4 Make a paste with flour and water. Tear the newspaper into strips and dip them into the paste. Cover the handle in the papier mâché strips.

5 Use newspaper to make the nose and ears. Add a strip of papier mâché at the top of the head for the crown. Let dry, then sandpaper until smooth.

6 Paint a base coat of gray paint on the face and bronze on the handle. Then add the details of the face and crown in black using a fine paintbrush.

7 Cut out a circle of reflective card stock to match the mirror shape. Glue the reflective card onto the white card stock. This is your bronze mirror.

Egyptian Crafts

The ancient Egyptians loved beautiful objects, and the craft items that have survived still amaze us today. There are shining gold rings and pendants, necklaces inlaid with glass and a dazzling blue glazed pottery called faience. Jars made of a smooth white stone called alabaster have been preserved in almost perfect condition, along with chairs and chests made of cedar wood imported from the Near East.

Egyptians made beautiful baskets and storage pots. Some pottery was made from river clay, but the finest pots were made from a chalky clay found at Quena. Pots were shaped by hand or, later, on a potter's wheel. Some were polished with a smooth pebble until their surface shone. We know so much about Egyptian craft work because many beautiful items were placed in tombs, so that the dead person could use them in the next world.

ALABASTER ART
Jars such as this would have held oils and perfumes. This elaborate jar was among the treasures in the tomb of King Tutankhamun (1334–1325 B.C.).

GLASS FISH
This beautiful striped fish looks as if it should be swimming in the reefs of the Red Sea. In fact, it is a glass jar used to store oils. Glass-making became popular in Egypt after 1500 B.C. The glass was made from sand and salty crystals. It would then have been colored with metals and shaped while still hot.

MAKE A LOTUS TILE

You will need: cardboard (2 sheets), pencil, ruler, scissors, self-drying clay, modeling tool, sand-paper acrylic paint (blue, gold, green, yellow ocher), water pot, brush. Optional: rolling pin, board.

1 Using the final picture as reference, draw both tile shapes onto cardboard. Cut them out. Draw the pattern of tiles onto the sheet of card and cut around the border.

2 Roll out the clay on a board with a rolling pin or bottle. Place the overall outline over the clay and carefully trim off the edges. Discard the extra clay.

3 Mark the individual tile patterns into the clay, following the outlines carefully. Cut through the lines, but do not separate them out yet.

DESERT RICHES

The dwellers of the green Nile valley feared and disliked the desert. They called it the Red Land. However, the deserts did provide them with great mineral wealth, including blue-green turquoise, purple amethyst, and blue agate.

blue agate   *turquoise*   *amethyst*

ROYAL TILES

Many beautiful Egyptian tiles have been discovered by archaeologists. It is thought that they were used to decorate furniture and floors in the palaces of the pharaohs.

TUTANKHAMUN'S WAR CHEST

Tutankhamun is in battle against the Syrians and the Nubians on this painted chest. On the lid, the young king is seen hunting in the desert. The incredible detail of the painting shows that this was the work of a very skilled artist. When Tutankhamun's tomb was opened, the chest was found to contain children's clothes. The desert air was so dry that neither the wood, leather nor fabric had rotted.

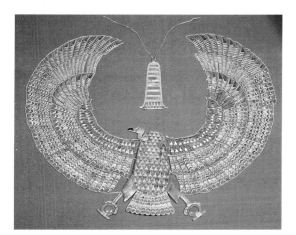

NEKHBET COLLAR

In this splendid collar, the spectacular wings of the vulture goddess Nekhbet include 250 feather sections made of colored glass set in gold. The vulture's beak and eye are made from a black, volcanic glass called obsidian. It was one of 17 collars found in Tutankhamun's tomb. As one of many amazing objects found in the young king's tomb, it shows us the incredible skill of Egyptian craftsmen.

4 Now use the tool to etch patterns of leaves and flowers into the surface of the soft clay, as shown. Separate the pieces and let them dry.

5 When one side of each tile has dried, turn it over. Let the other side dry. Then sand down the edges of the tiles until they are smooth.

6 The tiles are now ready for painting. Carefully paint the patterns in green, yellow ocher, gold, and blue. Leave them in a warm place to dry.

These tiles are similar to those found at a royal palace in Thebes. The design looks a lot like a lotus, the sacred waterlily of ancient Egypt.

Chinese Pottery

POTTERY MAKING developed in the Far East long before it was mastered in northwest Europe. More than 5,000 years ago, Chinese potters had worked out how to shape clay, and bake it in kilns (ovens) at temperatures of about 1650°F to make it hard. Gradually, they discovered how to bake better clays at much higher temperatures to make more hardwearing and water-resistant pottery, and to coat it with shiny, waterproof glazes. The toughest, most waterproof and most delicate ceramic of all was porcelain. This was invented by the Chinese about 800 years before it was produced in Europe. Porcelain was one of China's most important exports to Asia and Europe.

The Chinese were also the first to use lacquer, a smooth, hard varnish made from the sap of a tree. From about 1300 B.C., lacquer was used for coating wooden surfaces, such as house timbers, bowls, or furniture. It could also be applied to leather and metal. Natural lacquer is gray, but in China pigment was added to make it black or bright red. It was applied in many layers until thick enough to be carved or inlaid with mother-of-pearl.

ENAMEL WARE
Ming dynasty craft workers created this ornate flask. They made a design with thin metal wire, then filled the wire compartments with drops of colored, melted glass. The technique is called cloisonné.

FLORAL BOTTLE
This attractive Ming dynasty bottle is decorated with a coating of bright red lacquer. The lacquer is colored with a mineral called cinnabar. It would have taken many long hours to apply and dry the many layers of lacquer. The bottle is carved with a design of peonies, which were a very popular flower in China.

CHINA'S HISTORY TOLD ON THE BIG SCREEN
A beautifully detailed, glossy lacquer screen shows a group of Portuguese merchants on a visit to China. It was made in the 1600s. Chinese crafts first became popular in Europe at this time, as European traders began doing business in southern China's ports.

FISH ON A PLATE

Pictures of fish decorate the border of this precious porcelain plate. It was made during the reign of the Qing emperor Yongzheng (1722–1736), a period famous for its elegant designs. It is colored with enamel. Porcelain is made from a fine white clay called kaolin (china clay) and a mineral called feldspar. They are fired (baked) at a very high temperature.

A JUG OF WINE

An unknown Chinese potter made this beautiful wine jug about 1,000 years ago. It has been fired at such a high temperature that it has become strong and water-resistant. It was then coated with a gray-green glaze called celadon and fired again.

LIFE-LIKE FIGURES

A Ming dynasty entertainer smiles at his audience. All sorts of pottery figures have been found in Ming dynasty tombs. Potters made lively figures of merchants, musicians, court ladies, and animals. Some are comic, while others are beautiful.

DEEP BLUE, PURE WHITE

Blue-and-white vases are typical of the late Ming dynasty (1368–1644). In the 1600s, large numbers were exported to Europe. Many were produced at the imperial potteries at Jingdezhen, in northern Jiangxi province. The workshops were set up in 1369, as the region had plentiful supplies of the very best clay. Some of the finest pottery ever made was produced there in the 1400s and 1500s.

Fine Crafts in Japan

Tʜᴇʀᴇ ɪs ᴀ ʟᴏɴɢ ᴛʀᴀᴅɪᴛɪᴏɴ among Japanese craftworkers of making everyday things as beautiful as possible. Craftworkers created exquisite items for the wealthiest and most knowledgeable collectors. They used a wide variety of materials—pottery, metal, lacquer, cloth, paper, and bamboo. Pottery ranged from plain, simple earthenware to delicate porcelain painted with brilliantly colored glazes. Japanese metalworkers produced alloys (mixtures of metals) before they were known elsewhere in the world. Cloth was woven from fibers in elaborate designs. Bamboo and other plants from the grass family were woven into elegant *tatami* mats (floor mats) and containers of all different shapes and sizes. Japanese craftworkers also made beautifully decorated *inro* (little boxes, used like purses) which dangled from men's *kimono* sashes.

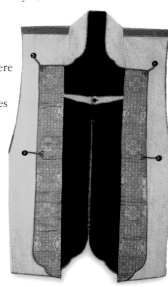

SHINY LACQUER
This samurai helmet was made for ceremonial use. It is covered in lacquer (varnish) and decorated with a diving dolphin. Producing shiny lacquerware was a slow process. An object was covered with many thin layers of lacquer. Each layer was allowed to dry, then polished, before more lacquer was applied. The lacquer could then be carved.

SAMURAI SURCOAT
Even the simplest garments were beautifully crafted. This surcoat (loose, sleeveless tunic) was made for a member of the noble Mori family, probably around 1800. Surcoats were worn by samurai on top of their armor.

MAKE A *NETSUKE* FOX
You will need: paper, pencil, ruler, self-drying clay, balsa wood, modeling tool, fine sandpaper, acrylic paint, paintbrush, water pot, darning needle, cord, small box (for an inro*), scissors, toggle, wide belt.*

1 Draw a square 2 x 2in. on a piece of paper. Roll out a ball of clay to the size of the square. Shape the clay so that it comes to a point at one end.

2 Turn your clay over. Lay a stick of balsa approximately 2½ in. long, along the back. Stick a thin sausage of clay over the stick. Press to secure.

3 Turn the clay over. Cut out two triangles of clay. Join them to the head using the tool. Make indentations to shape them into a fox's ears.

METALWORK

Craftworkers polish the sharp swords and knives they have made. It took many years of training to become a metalworker. Japanese craftsmen were famous for their fine skills at smelting and handling metals.

BOXES FOR BELTS

Inro were originally designed for storing medicines. The first *inro* were plain and simple, but after about 1700 they were often decorated with exquisite designs. These *inro* have been lacquered (coated with a shiny substance made from the sap of the lacquer tree). Inside, they contain several compartments stacked on top of each other.

MASTERWORK

This beautiful jar is decorated with a design of white flowers, painted over a shiny red and black glaze. It was painted by the master-craftsman Ogata Kenzan, who lived from 1663 to 1743.

Wear your inro *dangling from your belt. In early Japan,* inro *were usually worn by men. They were held in place with carved toggles called* netsuke.

4 Use the handle of your modeling tool to make your fox's mouth. Carve eyes, nostrils, teeth, and a frown line. Use the top of a pencil to make eye holes.

5 Let dry. Gently sand the *netsuke* and remove the balsa wood stick. Paint it with several layers of acrylic paint. Leave in a warm place to dry.

6 Thread cord through the four corners of a small box with a darning needle. Then thread the cord through a toggle and the *netsuke,* as shown.

7 Put a wide belt round your waist. Thread the *netsuke* under the belt. It should rest on the top of it. The *inro* (box) should hang down, as shown.

Roman Decoration

Uring the Roman era, houses and public places were decorated with paintings and statues. Mosaics were pictures made using *tesserae,* squares of stone, pottery, or glass, which were pressed into soft cement. Mosaic pictures might show hunting scenes, the harvest or Roman gods. Geometric patterns were often used as borders.

Wall paintings, or murals, often showed garden scenes, birds and animals or heroes and goddesses. They were painted onto wooden panels or directly onto the wall. Roman artists often tricked the eye by painting false columns, archways, and shelves. The Romans were skilled sculptors, using stone, marble, and bronze. They imitated the ancient Greeks in putting up marble statues in public places and gardens. These might be of gods and goddesses or emperors and generals.

A Country Scene
This man and wild boar are part of a mosaic made in Roman North Africa. Making a mosaic was quite tricky—a lot like doing a jigsaw puzzle. Even so, skilled artists could create lifelike scenes from cubes of colored glass, pottery, and stone.

Sculpture
Statues of metal or stone were often placed in gardens. This bronze figure is in the remains of a house in Pompeii. It is of a faun, a god of the countryside.

Floor Mosaics
Birds, animals, plants, and country scenes were popular subjects for mosaics. These parrots are part of a much larger, and quite elaborate, floor mosaic from a Roman house.

Make a Mosaic

You will need: rough paper, pencil, ruler, scissors, large sheet of cardboard, self-drying clay, rolling pin, wooden board, modeling knife, acrylic paints, paintbrush, water pot, clear varnish and brush (optional), plaster of Paris, spreader, muslin rag.

1 Sketch out your mosaic design on rough paper. Use a simple design like this one. Cut the cardboard so it measures 10 x 4 in. Copy the design onto it.

2 Roll out the clay on the board. Measure out small squares on the clay. Cut them out with the modeling knife. Let dry. These will be your tesserae.

3 Paint the pieces in batches of different colors. When the paint is dry, coat them with clear varnish for extra strength and shine. Let dry.

MOSAIC MATERIALS

Mosaics were often made inside frames, in workshops, and then transported to where they were to be used. Sometimes, the tesserae were brought to the site and fitted on the spot. The floor of an average room in a Roman town house might need more than 100,000 pieces.

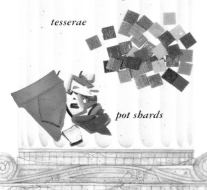

tesserae

pot shards

MUSICIANS AND DANCERS

This dramatic painting is on the walls of an excavated villa in Pompeii. It is one in a series of paintings that show the secret rites, or mysteries, honoring the Greek god of wine, Dionysus, who was called Bacchus in Rome.

REAL OR FAKE?

Roman artists liked to make painted objects appear real enough to touch. This bowl of fruit on a shelf is typical of this style of painting. It was found on the wall of a villa that belonged to a wealthy Roman landowner.

4 Spread the plaster of Paris onto the cardboard, a small part at a time. While it is still wet, press in your tesserae following the design, as shown above.

5 When the mosaic is dry, use the muslin rag to polish up the surface. Any other soft, dry cloth would also be suitable. Now your mosaic is ready for display.

The Romans liked to have mosaics in their homes. Wealthy people often had elaborate mosaics in their courtyards and dining rooms, as these were rooms that visitors would see.

Viking Picture Stories

T HE VIKINGS WERE SKILLED ARTISTS and metalworkers as well as fierce warriors, although they rarely painted pictures. Instead, they embroidered tapestries, and carved pictures on wooden panels or stones.

Viking art often recorded events. Pieces of tapestry found in a Viking ship burial site in Oseberg, in Norway, show a procession of horses and wagons. The tradition of making tapestries to tell stories and events was continued by the Normans, descendants of the Vikings who settled in Normandy, in France, in the 8th century A.D. More than 150 years later, the Bayeux Tapestry was made there. In 79 embroidered scenes, the Bayeux Tapestry told the story of the Norman conquest of England in 1066.

Many Viking artworks often describe the doom of the gods and destruction of the world in tales of great feuds and battles between gods, mythical monsters, and giants. These often show bold, powerful figures, intricate, swirling patterns, and graceful animals. They demonstrate the Viking artists' love of movement and line.

After the Viking Age, their style of art disappeared as Europeans brought different styles to the area.

TWILIGHT OF THE GODS
This stone carving from the Isle of Man shows the final battle of the gods. Odin, the father of the gods, is shown here armed with a spear and a raven on his shoulder. He is killed by Fenrir, the gray wolf.

ART FROM URNES
At Urnes, in Norway, there is a stave church that has old wood panels. They date from the final years of the Viking Age. This one shows a deer eating Yggdrasil, the tree that holds up the world. Urnes has given its name to the last and most graceful period of Viking art and design.

MAKE A SCARY FACE

You will need: pencil, paper, scissors, self-drying clay, rolling pin, work board, modeling tool, sandpaper, thick brush, acrylic paints, fine brush, water pot.

1 Draw a scary monster face on paper. Copy this one or one from a book, or make up your own. Make your drawing big and bold. Then cut it out.

2 Roll out a large piece of modeling clay into a slab. Use a modeling tool to trim off the edges to look like the uneven shape of a rune stone.

3 Lay your design on top of the clay slab. Use a modeling tool to go over the lines of your drawing, pushing through the paper into the clay.

WOLF BITES GOD

In the picture below, Tyr, god of the assemblies and lawmakers. His hand is being bitten off by Fenrir, the gray wolf. Fenrir is straining against a magic chain forged by the dwarfs. The chain is made from all kinds of impossible things, such as fish's breath and a mountain's roots. Tyr's name survives in the English word "Tuesday."

WHISTLE

This tiny whistle was made from a bird's leg bone. It may have been used to scare birds away from the crops.

WALL HANGING

The bold design on this tapestry shows the gods Odin, Thor, and Frey. It comes from a church in Sweden and dates from the 1100s, just after the Viking Age. It is probably similar to the wall hangings woven for royal halls in the earlier Viking times.

4 Go over all the lines in the picture. Make sure the lines show up on the clay below. Remove the paper to see the monster's outline in clay.

5 Let the clay dry, turning it over to make sure it is well aired. When it is hard, smooth it down with fine sandpaper, then brush with a paintbrush.

6 Now paint the face as shown, using yellow ocher, black, red, and blue. Let each color dry completely before starting the next. Let dry.

Here's a face to scare off evil spirits on a dark night! Faces like this, with interlacing beard and mustache, appeared on stone memorials in the Viking Age.

Sport and Games in China

FROM EARLY IN CHINA'S history, kings and nobles loved to go hunting for pleasure. Horses and chariots were used to hunt deer and wild boar. Dogs and even cheetahs were trained to chase the prey. Spears, bows, and arrows were then used to kill it. Falconry (using birds of prey to hunt animals) was commonplace by about 2000 B.C.

In the Ming and Qing dynasties ancient spiritual disciplines used by Daoist monks were brought together with the battle training used by warriors. These martial arts (*wu shu*) were intended to train both mind and body. They came to include the body movements known as tai chi (*taijiquan*), sword play (*jianwu*) and the extreme combat known as kung fu (*gongfu*).

Archery was a popular sport in imperial China. The Chinese also loved gambling, and may have invented the first card games more than 2,000 years ago.

CHINESE CHESS
The traditional Chinese game of xiang qi is similar to western chess. One army battles against another, with round discs used as playing pieces. To tell the discs apart, each is marked with a name.

pieces

xiang qi board

PEACE THROUGH MOVEMENT
A student of tai chi practices his art. The Chinese first developed the system of exercises known as tai chi more than 2,000 years ago. The techniques of tai chi were designed to help relax the human body and concentrate the mind.

MAKE A KITE

You will need: 12in. wooden skewers (x12), ruler, scissors, glue and brush, plastic insulating tape, 34 x 22 in. white paper, pencil, paint (blue, red, yellow, black and pink), paintbrush, water pot, string, piece of wooden dowel, small metal ring.

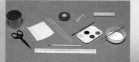

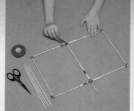

1 Make a 15¾ x 11¾ in. rectangle by joining some of the sticks. Overlap the sticks for strength, then glue and tape together. Add a center rod.

2 Make another rectangle 6 x 15¾ in. long. Overlay the second rectangle on top of the first one. Tape rectangles together, as shown above.

3 Place frame onto a sheet of white 34 x 22 in. paper. Draw a 1 in. border around outside of frame. Add curves around the end of the center rod.

ALL-IN WRESTLING

This bronze figure of two wrestling muscle men was made in about 300 B.C. Wrestling was a very popular entertainment and sport in imperial China. It continues to be an attraction at country fairs and festivals.

BAMBOO BETTING

Gamblers place bets in a game of *liu po*. Bamboo sticks were thrown like dice to decide how far the counters on the board should move. Gambling was a widespread pastime during the Han dynasty. People would bet large sums of money on the outcome of card games, horse races, and cockfights.

POLO PONIES

These women from the Tang dynasty are playing a fast and furious game of polo. They are probably noblewomen from the Emperor's royal court. The sport of polo was originally played in India and central Asia. It was invented as a training game to improve the riding skills of soldiers in cavalry units.

Chinese children today still play with homemade paper kites. Kites were invented in China in about 400 B.C.

4 Cut out the kite shape from the paper. Using a pencil, draw the details of your dragon design on the paper. Paint in your design and let dry.

5 Cut a triangular piece of paper to hang from the end of your kite as a tail. Fold tail over rod at bottom of kite, as shown. Tape tail into position.

6 Carefully tape and glue your design onto the frame. Fold over border that you allowed for when cutting out the paper. Tape to back of paper, as shown.

7 Wrap 30 ft. of string around dowel. Tie other end to ring. Pass 2 pieces of string through kite from the back. Tie to center rod. Tie other ends to ring.

Popular Music in Ancient Greece

MUSIC AND DANCE WERE important parts of Greek life. People sang, played, and danced at religious ceremonies. Music was enjoyed for pleasure and entertainment at family celebrations, dramatic performances, feasts, and drinking parties. Few written records remain of the notes played, but examples of the instruments do. The most popular instruments were the pipes. They were wind instruments similar to the oboe or clarinet. One pipe on its own was called the *aulos*, two played together were known as *auloi*. The stringed lyre and flute were other popular instruments. The stringed lyre produced solemn and dignified music. It was often played by men of noble birth to accompany a poetry recital. The flute was more commonly played by slaves or dancing girls.

BREATH CONTROL
The leather strap tied around the auloi-player's cheeks helped to focus the power of his breath. One tube of the auloi supplied the melody, while the other produced an accompanying drone to give more depth to the sound. The aulos had as few as three or as many as 24 fingerholes for making the different notes.

Greek soldiers complained that lack of music was a hardship of war. Spartan soldiers resolved this problem by blowing tunes on pipes as they marched. Music was believed to have magical powers. Greek legend tells of Orpheus soothing savage beasts by playing his lyre. Another myth tells how Amphion (a son of Zeus) made stones move on their own and built a wall around the city of Thebes, by playing his lyre.

BANG! CRASH!
The bronze figurine above is playing the cymbals. They made a sound similar to castanets. The Greeks used the cymbals to accompany dancing. Other percussion instruments included wooden clappers and hand-held drums, like tambourines.

TIMPANON
You will need: scissors, corrugated cardboard, tape measure, plate, white card stock, compass, pencil, white glue, tape, strips of newspaper, cream paper, red and purple felt-tip pens, ochre card stock, red and yellow ribbons.

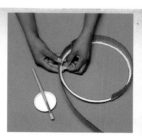

1 Cut out a strip of corrugated cardboard 2 in. wide. Wrap it around a dinner plate. Add 2½ in. on to the length of this cardboard and cut it off.

2 Put the plate upside down on the white card stock. Draw around it. Draw another circle 1¼ in. inside the first. Cut this out to make a ring.

3 Glue the cardboard strip that you made in step 1 to the edge of the card stock ring you made in step 2. Then tape them together for extra hold.

DIVINE MUSIC

Terpsichore was one of the Nine Muses, or spirits of the arts. She was the spirit of dance and music. Here Terpsichore plays a harp while her attendants hold the lyre and auloi. Other Muses included Polyhymnia, the spirit of hymns, and Euterpe, the spirit of flute-playing.

PERCUSSION

The timpanon was a tambourine made of animal skin, stretched over a frame. It was tapped to provide rhythmic accompaniment at dances or recitals. Stringed and wind instruments were thought superior because they made fitting music for solemn or exclusive occasions. Drums, cymbals and clappers were associated with buskers.

ENTERTAINING

In this plate painting a young man plays the auloi while his female companion dances. Professional musicians were often hired to entertain guests at dinner parties. Sometimes the musicians were household slaves.

To play the timpanon tap on it with your fingers, as the ancient Greeks would have done.

4 Mix some papier mâché solution with 1 part glue to 2 parts water. Soak strips of newspaper in it and cover the card stock ring with the wet strips.

5 Draw around the plate onto cream paper. Draw another circle 2 in. outside this. To make tabs, cut out about 28 small triangles around the edge.

6 Draw the design shown above onto the paper. Place the paper over the top of the card stock ring. Dab glue on each tab and stick onto the corrugated card.

7 Cut a strip of ochre card stock to fit around the timpanon. Decorate it as above and glue on. Make 4 bows with the ribbons and glue around the edge.

Mythical Tales of Greece

Greek mythology is rich in stories of victorious heroes and heroines, quarreling gods and goddesses, and mysterious and unusual creatures. While keeping people entertained, the stories also tried to answer questions about how the world and humans came into existence. These powerful tales provided inspiration for ancient Greek art and material for their plays, which were performed to audiences of more than 10,000. In addition, they were a valuable historical record and encouraged the Greeks to take pride in their cultural past.

Traditionally, mythical stories were passed down generations by word of mouth. Sometimes traveling bards were paid to recite poems, which they had learned by heart. Eventually, these tales came to be written down. The earliest of these that survive are thought to be the work of the poet Homer (*c.*800 B.C.). Two poems that we know about are *The Odyssey* and *The Iliad*. Both tell tales of heroes battling against supernatural forces.

Monster Killer

According to Greek legend the Minotaur was half-bull and half-man. It lived in a maze called the labyrinth on the island of Crete. Many people had entered the maze but never came out. Each year the people of Athens were forced to send human sacrifices to feed the bull. The hero Theseus made it his mission to kill the Minotaur. A princess presented Theseus with a sword and a ball of string to help him. Theseus unwound the string as he walked through the maze. After killing the Minotaur he followed the string back to the entrance of the cave.

Snake Strangler

The super-strong Heracles was the only human being to become a Greek god. This Roman fresco shows him as a baby strangling serpents sent by the jealous goddess Hera to kill him.

Head of Medusa

You will need: board, self-drying modeling clay, rolling pin, ruler, modeling tool, pencil, sandpaper, acrylic paints, one small and one large paintbrush, varnish (1 part water to 1 part white glue).

1 With a rolling pin, roll out a slab of clay 8 x 8 in. and ¼ in. thick. With the modeling tool, cut out a head in the shape shown in the picture.

2 Shape a small piece of clay into a nose. Mold it onto the head with your fingers. Use the modeling tool to smooth the edges into the face.

3 Carve a mouth with lots of teeth and two eyes and etch a gruesome design into the head. Press the end of a pencil into the eyes to make eyeballs.

STONY STARE

Medusa was a winged monster with hair of snakes. She was one of three such female gorgons. Medusa had a face so horrific that any human who looked directly at it was turned to stone. The only way to kill her was to cut off her head. Medusa, whose name means "cunning," outwitted several would-be killers. The hero Perseus finally killed her with help from Athena and Hermes. They lent Perseus a magic cap to make him invisible, a sickle to cut off Medusa's head and a shield in which to see her reflection. Even dead, Medusa remained powerful. Perseus killed his enemy Polydectes by forcing him to look at her face.

FOOLING THE GIANT

King Odysseus was a mythical hero who had many adventures. One escapade found him captured in a cave by a one-eyed giant. To escape, Odysseus stabbed out the giant's eye and rode out of the cave clinging to the underside of a ram.

The word gorgon in Greek suggests the monster's glaring eyes.

FLYING HORSE

The winged horse Pegasus appeared on the coins of Corinth as the city's symbol. Pegasus helped Bellerophon, a Corinthian hero, in his battles. First against the Chimaera which was a monster with a lion's head, a goat's middle and a snake's tail and then against the Amazons, a race of female warriors.

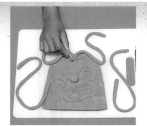

4 Between the palms of your hands, roll out four thin strips of clay to represent the snakes on Medusa's head. Press them into place as shown above.

5 Press a finger down on the end of each roll to make a snake's head. Use the modeling tool and pencil to carve in scales on the snakes' bodies.

6 The head needs to dry completely before you can paint the face. To dry it, let it sit for a few hours on either side. Be careful when you turn it over.

7 When the head is completely dry, sand with fine sandpaper. Paint the face in black, red, white, and gold as shown here. Let dry and varnish.

Roman Sport and Combat

MOST ROMANS preferred watching sport to taking part. There were some, however, who enjoyed athletics and keeping fit. They took their exercise at the public baths and at the sports ground or *palaestra*. Men competed at wrestling, the long jump, and swimming. Women also exercised by working out with weights.

Boxing matches and chariot races were always well attended. The races took place on a long, oval racetrack, called a circus. The crowds watched with such excitement that violent riots often followed. Charioteers and their teams became big stars. Roman crowds also enjoyed watching displays of violence. Bloody battles between gladiators and fights among wild animals took place in a special oval arena, called an amphitheater. Roman entertainments became more spectacular and bloodthirsty with time. The arenas of amphitheaters were sometimes flooded for mock sea battles.

A COLOSSEUM
This is the colosseum in the Roman city of El Djem, in Tunisia. A colosseum was a kind of amphitheater. Arenas such as this were built all over the Empire. The largest and most famous is the Colosseum in Rome.

DEATH OR MERCY?
Gladiators usually fought to the death, but a wounded gladiator could appeal for mercy. The excited crowd would look for the emperor's signal. A thumbs-up meant his life was spared. A thumbs-down meant he must die.

COME ON YOU REDS!

Charioteers belonged to teams and wore their team's colors when they raced. Some also wore protective leather helmets, like the one in this mosaic. In Rome, there were four teams—the Reds, Blues, Whites, and Greens. Each team had faithful fans, and charioteers were every bit as popular as football stars today.

A DAY AT THE RACES

This terra-cotta carving records an exciting moment at the races. Chariot racing was a passion for most Romans. Chariots were usually pulled by four horses, though just two or as many as six could be used. Accidents and foul play were common as the chariots thundered around the track.

THE CHAMP

Boxing was a deadly sport. Fighters, like this boxer, wore studded thongs instead of padded boxing gloves. Severe injuries, and even brain damage, were probably quite common.

THE GREEK IDEAL

The Romans admired all things Greek, including their love of athletics. This painted Greek vase dates from about 333 B.C. and shows long-distance runners. However, Roman crowds were not interested in athletic contests in the Greek style, such as the Olympic Games.

American Indian Storytelling

NORTH AMERICAN INDIANS LOVED storytelling. Many stories taught the children to respect nature and animals, or described social behavior. Stories were also a way of passing on tribal customs, rituals, and religious beliefs. Some tribes considered it unlucky to tell tales of mythological events during the summer months. They looked forward to the long winter nights when they would gather in their tipis or lodges and huddle around the fire. Then, they listened to the storyteller who was often one of the elders. A story might recall past hunts and battles, or it could be complete fiction, although the listener could never be sure as the tales were always embellished. This was especially true if the storyteller was from the Yuma tribe. The Great Dreams of the Yuma people were fantastic tales, usually performed as plays and often based on tribal rituals and folklore.

SCROLL RECORDS
This is a fine example of a birchbark scroll. It is a Midewiwin (Grand Medicine Society) record of the Ojibwa. Most ceremonies were so long and complicated that a chart had to be made to remember all the songs and prayers in the right order. A document such as this was used to record the history and initiation rites of a tribe. Without it, knowledge of them might be lost forever.

STORY BEHIND THE PICTURES
A proud Mandan chief and his wife pose for a picture to be painted. It is not just the chief's headdress that reveals great prowess in battle. The painted skin displayed by the woman tells stories of the tribe's history. The war scenes show that the tribe has been involved in many victorious battles in the past. This group picture was painted between 1833 and 1835 by George Catlin. He was an artist whose paintings of North American Indians are themselves a form of storytelling. They are an important source of information about tribal lives, customs, and dress, particularly since the Indians at that time did not write any books about themselves.

COLORED SAND

Although many tribes made sandpaintings *(shown above)* it was the Navajo who developed the art. The painter trickled powders of yellow, white, and red ocher, and sandstone into patterns on the sand. Each picture described humans and spirits connected with creation stories and was usually used as part of a healing ceremony.

HEROIC TALES

The Sioux chief, seen at the bottom of this picture, must have been exceptionally brave since his headdress is very long. Painting warrior shields was an ancient art used to pass on tales of battle heroics. This shield may have been painted by one of the warriors involved. Shields were kept in the lodge and brought out when the warrior retold how brave he was. It would be given to his children to keep his memory alive.

WRITTEN IN STONE

These children are reading about the history of their ancestors in Colorado Springs. Stone Age North American Indians (the early Pueblo people) carved animals and designs on stone, which told a little of their way of life.

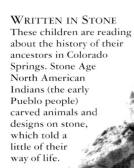

THE HISTORIAN

A young boy looks on as his father records tribal stories on dried animal hide. He is already learning the importance of recording the family history. Even in 1903, when this picture was painted, many tribes used picture writing, not the printed word of the white man.

STORY OF LIFE

Totem poles such as this were found mainly on the Northwest Coast. Generally they were carved out of trunks of thuja (red cedar trees) and told tribal or family history. Each face was a mythical creature, an animal protector. Frontal poles stood against Haida homes displaying the crests of the families who lived inside.

Celtic Bards and Musicians

THE CELTS ENJOYED MUSIC, poems and songs as entertainment, and for more serious purposes. Music accompanied Celtic warriors into battle and made them feel brave. Poems praised the achievements of a great chieftain or the adventures of bold raiders, and recorded the history of a tribe. Dead chieftains and heroes, and possibly even ordinary people, too, were mourned with sad laments. On special occasions, and in the homes of high-ranking Celts, poems and songs were performed by people called bards.

Roman writers described the many years of training to become a bard. Bards learned how to compose using all the different styles of poetry, and memorized hundreds of legends and songs. They also learned how to play an instrument, and to read and write, although most Celtic music and poetry was never written down. Becoming a bard was the first step towards being a druid (priest).

HOLY MUSIC
We do not know what part music played in Celtic religious ceremonies, but it was probably important. This stone statue shows a Celtic god playing a lyre. The Celts believed that religious knowledge, and music, was too holy to be written down. Sadly, this means that many Celtic poems and songs have been lost forever.

GRACEFUL DANCER
Naked dancing girls may have entertained guests at important feasts. This little bronze statue, just 5 in. high, dates from around 50 B.C. The Celts enjoyed dancing, and from the evidence of this statue it seems likely that their dances were very wild in their movements.

MAKE A HARP
You will need: card stock 15 x 19¼ in., pencil, ruler, scissors, cardboard 15 x 19¼ in., felt-tip pen, paints, paintbrushes, awl, colored string, paper fasteners.

1 On the piece of card stock, draw a diagonal line from corner to corner. Draw a second, gently curving line, shaped at one end, as shown.

2 Draw two lines (*a* and *b*), 1¾ in. in from the edge of the paper. Join them with a curved line *c*. Finally add a curved line *d* parallel to *a*, as shown.

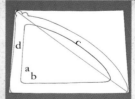

3 Cut out the harp shape. Place it on cardboard. Carefully draw around it with a felt-tip pen both inside and out. Cut the cardboard harp out.

HARPIST

This harpist is pictured on the Dupplin Cross, from Scotland. The harp itself is large and triangular in shape. It was placed on the ground and held between the harpist's knees. Such harps were popular at the end of the Celtic period.

MUSICAL GROUP

Musicians are shown playing at a religious ceremony on this stone carving from Scotland, dating from around A.D. 900. The bottom panel shows a harpist plucking the strings of his harp, while a fellow musician plays a pipe. In the foreground is a drum, possibly made from a barrel with a skin stretched over it.

INSPIRED BY A DREAM

While a Celtic bard sleeps, he dreams of a beautiful woman from the world of the spirits. She will be the subject of his next song. Dreams and visions were a common theme in many ancient Celtic poems and legends. For example, Oisin, son of the great hero Finn MacCool, ran away with Niamh of the Golden Hair. Niamh was a spirit who appeared to Finn in a dream and invited him to come to a magic land across the waves.

Most Celtic poetry was not spoken, but sung or chanted to the music of a harp or a lyre. Bards used the music to create the right atmosphere to accompany their words, and to add extra dramatic effects, such as shivery sounds during a scary ghost tale.

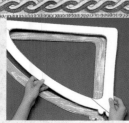

4 Glue one side of the card stock and one side of the cardboard. Stick them together. Paint the harp brown and leave it in a warm place to dry.

5 Use an awl to make holes approximately 2 in. apart along the two straight sides of the harp. These will be the holes for the strings.

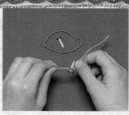

6 Cut a length of string 15¾ in. long. Cut 7 more pieces of string each 2 in. shorter than the last. Tie a paper fastener to both ends of each string.

7 Push the paper fasteners into the harp frame so that the strings lie diagonally across the harp. Adjust the strings so that they are stretched tightly.

PATOLLI

A group of Aztecs are shown here playing the game of *patolli*. It was played by moving dried beans or clay counters along a cross-shaped board with 52 squares. It could be very exciting. Players often bet on the result.

Games in Mesoamerica

MESOAMERICAN PEOPLE of Central America enjoyed sports and games after work and on festival days. Two favorite games were *tlachtli* or *ulama*, the famous Mesoamerican ball game, and *patolli*, a board game. The ball game was played in front of huge crowds, while *patolli* was a quieter game. Mesoamerican games were not just for fun. Both the ball game and *patolli* had religious meanings. In the first, the court symbolized the world, and the rubber ball stood for the Sun as it made its daily journey across the sky. Players were meant to keep the ball moving in order to give energy to the Sun. Losing teams were sometimes sacrificed as offerings to the Sun god. In *patolli*, the movement of counters on the board represented the passing years.

THE ACROBAT

This Olmec statue shows a very supple acrobat. Mesoamericans admired youth, fitness, and beauty. Sports were fun, but they could also be good training for the demands of war. Being fit was considered attractive.

FLYING MEN

Volador was a ceremony performed on religious festival days. Four men, dressed as birds and attached to ropes, jumped off a high pole. As they spun around, falling toward the ground, they circled the pole 13 times each. That made 52 circuits—the length of the Mesoamerican holy calendar cycle.

PLAY PATOLLI

You will need: thick cardboard, pencil, ruler, black marker pen, paints, small paintbrush, water pot, colored paper, scissors, white glue and glue brush, dried beans, self-drying clay.

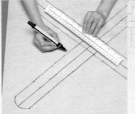

1 Measure a square of cardboard about 19¾ x 19¾ in. Using a ruler and a marker pen, draw three lines from corner to corner to make a cross-shape.

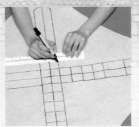

2 Draw seven pairs of spaces along each arm. The third space in from the end should be a double space. Paint triangles in it.

3 Draw eight jaguar heads and eight marigolds on differently colored paper. Cut them out. Paint the face of the Sun god into the center.

ALL DRESSED UP

A man dressed to play the Mesoamerican ballgame is shown in this terra-cotta statue. The figure was made around A.D. 800 on the Maya island of Jaina, off the western coast of the Yucatan peninsula. He wears a protective belt of leather and wood, padded wrist-guards and knee-guards, a pointed cap and big earrings. Being a ball-game player was risky but could bring rich rewards. Winners were sometimes allowed to claim the spectators' clothes and jewels as prizes.

TARGET RING

This stone ring comes from Chichen-Itza. Ball-game players used only their hips and knees to hit a solid rubber ball through rings like this fixed high on the ball-court walls.

PLAY BALL

The ruins of a huge ball-court can still be seen in the Maya city of Uxmal. The biggest courts were up to 65½ yards long and were built next to temples, in the center of cities. People crowded inside the court to watch. Play was fast, furious, and dangerous. Many players were injured as they clashed with opponents.

4 Stick the jaguars and marigolds randomly on the board. Paint a blue circle at the end of one arm, and a crown at the opposite end. Repeat in green on the other arms.

5 Paint five dried beans black with a white dot on one side. The beans will be thrown as dice. Make two counters from clay. Paint one green and one blue.

Most of the original rules for patolli have been lost. In this version, start each counter on the circle of the same color. The aim is to move your counter to the crown of the same color and back. Lose a turn if you land on a jaguar and get an extra turn if you land on a marigold.

At the Theater in Japan

GOING TO THE THEATER and listening to music were popular in Japan among the wealthy. There were several kinds of Japanese drama. They developed from religious dances at temples and shrines, or from slow, stately dances performed at the emperor's court.

Noh is the oldest form of Japanese drama. It developed in the 1300s from rituals and dances that had been performed for centuries before. Noh plays were serious and dignified. The actors performed on a bare stage, with only a backdrop. They chanted or sang their words, accompanied by drums and a flute. Noh performances were traditionally held in the open air, often at a shrine.

Kabuki plays were first seen around 1600. In 1629, the shoguns banned women performers and so male actors took their places. Kabuki plays became very popular in the new, fast-growing towns.

GRACEFUL PLAYER
This woman entertainer is holding a *shamisen*—a three-stringed instrument, played by plucking the strings. The *shamisen* often formed part of a group, together with a *koto* (zither) and flute.

POPULAR PUPPETS
Bunraku (puppet plays) originated about 400 years ago, when *shamisen* music, dramatic chanting and hand-held puppets were combined. The puppets were so large and complex that it took three men to move them around on stage.

NOH THEATER MASK
You will need: tape measure, balloon, newspaper, bowl, glue, petroleum jelly, pin, scissors, felt-tip pen, modeling clay, awl, paints (red, yellow, black, and white), paintbrush, water pot, cord.

1 Ask a friend to measure around your head above the ears. Blow up a balloon to fit this measurement. This will be the base for the papier mâché.

2 Rip up strips of newspaper. Soak in a water and glue mixture (1 part glue to 2 parts water). Cover the balloon with a layer of petroleum jelly.

3 Cover the front and sides of your balloon with a layer of papier mâché. Let dry. Repeat 2 or 3 times. When dry, pop the balloon.

TRAGIC THEATER
An audience watches a scene from an outdoor performance of a Noh play. Noh drama was always about important and serious topics. Favorite subjects were death and the afterlife, and the plays were often very tragic.

LOUD AND FAST
Kabuki plays were a complete contrast to Noh. They were fast-moving, loud, flashy, and very dramatic. Audiences admired the skills of the actors as much as the cleverness or thoughtfulness of the plots.

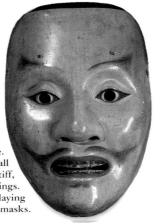

Put on your mask and feel like an actor in an ancient Noh play. Imagine that you are wearing his long, swirling robes, too.

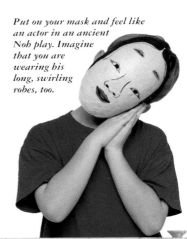

BEHIND THE MASK
This Noh mask represents a warrior's face. Noh drama did not try to be lifelike. The actors all wore masks and moved very slowly using stiff, stylized gestures to express their feelings. Noh plays were all performed by men. Actors playing women's parts wore female clothes and masks.

4 Trim the papier mâché so that it forms a mask shape. Ask a friend to mark where your eyes, nose, and mouth are when you hold it to your face.

5 Cut out the face holes with scissors. Put clay beneath the side of the mask at eye level. Use an awl to make two holes on each side.

6 Paint the face of a calm young lady from Noh theater on your mask. Use this picture as your guide. The mask would have been worn by a man.

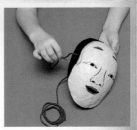

7 Fit the cord through the holes at each side. Tie one end. Once you have adjusted the mask so that it fits, tie the other end.

Entertaining Royal India

MUSIC AND DANCE have long entertained noble people in the royal courts. In Mughal India (1526–1857), courtiers listened to poetry and music every day. They loved riddles and word games, and in contests, poets were given half a verse and asked to complete it. Different art forms were connected to one another. For example, the *Natyashastra*, an ancient text on dance and drama, includes a long section on music. Dancers were also storytellers, using hand gestures to show meaning. North and south India developed their own musical traditions—Hindustani in the north and Karnatak in the south. Islam introduced new instruments, such as the sitar (a stringed instrument) and the tabla (a drum). Outside the courts, religion played a part in the development of singing. Muslim mystics sang and played musical pieces called *qawwali*, while Hindus sang songs to the god, Krishna.

JOYFUL OCCASION
Drummers and trumpeters at the Mughal court joyfully proclaim the birth of Emperor Akbar's son, Prince Salim. Music was often used to announce celebrations. Though they enjoyed royal patronage and were often renowned for their talent, musicians, dancers and actors were generally considered to be of low social standing.

INSTRUMENTAL BIRD
An instrument called a *sarongi* has been finely carved in the shape of a peacock. The *sarongi* was played with a bow and usually accompanied the dance performances of courtesans during late Mughal times.

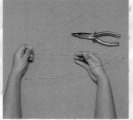

MAKE A PAIR OF ANKLETS
You will need: measuring tape, gardening wire, pliers, strips of red felt fabric, scissors, glue or adhesive tape, darning needle, strong thread, silver bells.

1 Measure the diameter of your ankle. Multiply this figure by three, then add 1½ in. for a loop. Use the pliers to cut two pieces of wire to this length.

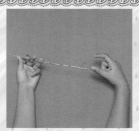

2 Loop the first cut piece of wire around itself about three times. Twist it tightly as you go. Then twist the second piece of wire in the same way.

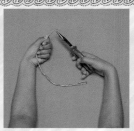

3 Using the pliers, bend one end of each strip of twisted wire to form a loop. Bend the other end to form a hook. These act as a fastener.

FOLK DANCING
This tapestry shows a folk dance in the Punjab. Folk dances were common in the villages, among ordinary people. Each dance usually involved lots of performers. People danced to celebrate births, weddings and many other special occasions.

ON A STRING
A woman from Rajasthan plays with a yo-yo. Games with balls and strings were not expensive, so they could be enjoyed by both rich and poor people. Many other kinds of games were afforded only by the wealthy.

ENTERTAINING AT COURT
Dancers perform the style of dance known as a Kathak for the great Mughal emperor Akbar. Dance was a popular form of entertainment at court. Many of the complicated dance styles known in India today originated at the courts of kings in ancient times. The dances performed at court often told a story.

Anklets were worn by dancers who performed at ceremonies in the royal courts of the Mughals.

4 Cut out two strips of felt fabric that are slightly longer than your strips of wire. Glue or tape a felt strip onto the end of the twisted wire.

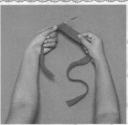

5 Wrap the felt around the wire, overlapping the edges of the felt. Glue the end of the felt to the place where you began. Wrap the second wire strip.

6 Thread a darning needle with sewing thread. Sew lots of tiny silver bells to the felt fabric covering your wire loops.

7 Repeat your stitches several times to make sure that the bells stay firmly in place. Add more bells, so that you cover both anklets completely.

Picture-writing in Mesopotamia

CLAY TABLET
Writing was done on clay tablets with a stylus (pen) made from a reed. The writer pressed the stylus into a slab of damp clay. This was left to dry and harden. The clay tablet in the picture, from around 3000 B.C., has symbols on it. One symbol looks like a hand and others resemble trees or plants. It is not clear which language they represent, although it is likely to be Sumerian.

WRITING, AS A MEANS of recording information, first developed in the ancient worlds of Mesopotamia (present-day Iraq), Egypt, and China. The earliest examples are about 5,000 years old and come from the Sumerian city-state of Uruk. At first, writing was in the form of pictures and numbers. It was used to make lists of produce such as barley, wine, and cheese, or numbers of cattle and donkeys. Gradually, this picture-writing was replaced by groups of wedge-shaped strokes formed by a reed pen as it was pressed into the clay. This type of writing is called cuneiform, which means "wedge-shaped." To begin with, cuneiform was only used to write Sumerian, but later it was adapted to write several other languages, including Assyrian, and Babylonian.

TWO SCRIBES
The scribe on the right is writing on a clay tablet with a stylus. He is making a list of all the booty and prisoners that his king has captured in battle. He is writing in Akkadian, one of the languages used by the Assyrians. The other scribe is writing on a leather roll, possibly in Aramaic, another language the Assyrians used. Aramaic was an easier language to write because it used an alphabet unlike Akkadian, which used about 600 different signs.

SHAPES AND SIZES
Differently shaped clay tablets, including prisms and cylinders, were used for writing. Many tablets were flat but some were three-dimensional and hollow like vases. One like this, that narrows at each end, is called a prism. It is about 12 inches long and records the military campaigns of King Sargon of Assyria.

A CLAY TABLET

You will need: pen, stiff cardboard, ruler, scissors, modeling clay, cutting board, rolling pin, blunt knife, paper, paint and paintbrush, cloth.

1 Draw a pointed stylus 8 x ½ in. onto the stiff cardboard with the pen. Use the shape in the picture as a guide. Cut the shape out with the scissors.

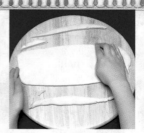

2 Roll out the clay on the cutting board with the rolling pin until it measures about 11¾ x 6 in. Use the knife to cut out the clay as shown.

3 Take your card stylus and start writing cuneiform script on your clay tablet. Use the wedge shape of your stylus to make the strokes.

COMMUNICATING IDEAS

Cuneiform signs gradually came to be used for ideas as well as objects. At first, a drawing of a head meant simply "head," but later came to mean "front" and "first." The symbols also came to represent spoken sounds and could be used to make new words. For example, in English, you could make the word "belief" by drawing the symbols for a bee and a leaf. The chart shows how cuneiform writing developed. On the top row are simple drawings. In the middle row the pictures have been replaced by groups of wedges, and in the bottom row are the even more simplified versions of the signs.

| anse donkey | gu ox | gisimmar date-palm | se barley | sag head |

The tablet you have made is about half the size of the original. Flat tablets were used for everything from scholarly works on medicine and mathematics to dictionaries and stories. The Epic of Gilgamesh took up 12 large tablets. Letters were written on tiny tablets.

WRITING ON THE ROCK FACE

Henry Rawlinson, a British army officer who helped decipher cuneiform in the mid-1800s, risks his life climbing a cliff face at Behistun to copy the writing there. The inscription was in three languages, Old Persian, Elamite, and Babylonian (Akkadian). He guessed that the cuneiform signs in Old Persian represented letters of the alphabet and found the name of Darius, the King of Persia. This helped scholars work out all three languages.

4 Copy the wedge-shapes of the cuneiform script shown here. See how each group of strokes combines to make a particular letter or word.

5 Move your tablet onto a piece of clean paper. Take the paintbrush and paint and cover the clay, working the paint well into the cuneiform script.

6 When the painting is finished, wipe across the clay with the cloth. Most of the paint should come off, leaving the lettering a darker color.

7 Let the clay and paint dry. The lettering on your finished tablet will read:
Nebuchadnezzar
King of Babylon.

Decoding Egyptian Script

MOST OF WHAT WE KNOW about the people of the past comes from the written language they left behind. Inscriptions providing information about the ancient Egyptians can be found on everything from obelisks to tombs. From 3100 B.C. the Egyptians used pictures called hieroglyphs. Each picture stood for an object, an idea, or a sound. There were around 1,000 hieroglyphic symbols. The term hiero means sacred. This is because it was initially used by the Egyptians for religious texts.

By 1780 B.C., hieroglyphs had evolved into hieratic, a more flowing text. In the latter days of ancient Egypt, an even simpler script called demotic (popular) was used. By A.D. 600, long after the last of the pharaohs, no one understood hieroglyphs. The secrets of ancient Egypt were lost for 1,200 years, until the discovery of the Rosetta Stone.

THE ROSETTA STONE

The discovery of the Rosetta Stone was a lucky accident. In 1799, a French soldier discovered a piece of stone at an Egyptian village called el-Rashid or Rosetta. On the stone, the same words were written in three scripts representing two languages. Hieroglyphic text is at the top, demotic text is in the center, and Greek is at the bottom.

EGYPTIAN CODE CRACKED

French scholar Jean-François Champollion cracked the Rosetta Stone code in 1822. The stone contains a royal decree written in 196 B.C. when the Greek king Ptolemy V was in power in Egypt. The Greek on the stone enabled Champollion to translate the hieroglyphs. This one discovery is central to our understanding of the way the ancient Egyptians used to live.

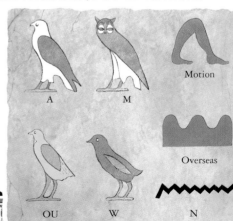

A

M

Motion

OU

W

N

Overseas

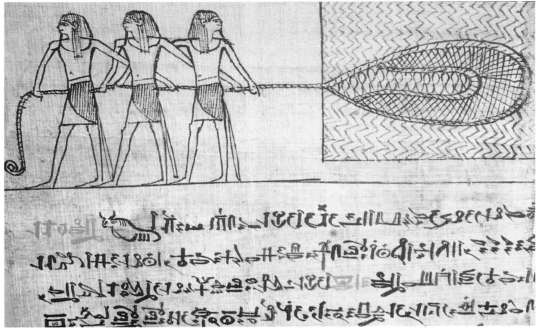

HIERATIC SCRIPT

The picture symbols of hieroglyphs, developed into hieratic script (above), which had signs that were more like letters. This script was more flowing and could be written quickly. It was used for writing stories, letters, and business contracts. It was always read from right to left.

DEMOTIC SCRIPT

A new script, demotic (*left*), was introduced towards the end of the New Kingdom (1550–1070 B.C.). This could be written even more quickly than hieratic script. Initially it was used for business, but soon it was also being used for religious and scientific writings. It disappeared when Egypt came under Roman rule in 30 B.C.

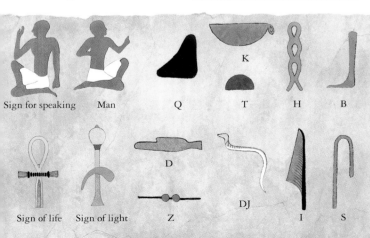

Sign for speaking   Man   Q   K   T   H   B

Sign of life   Sign of light   Z   D   DJ   I   S

HIEROGLYPHS

Made up of small pictures, hieroglyphs were based on simplified sketches of birds and snakes, plants, parts of the body, boats, and houses. Some hieroglyphs represented complete ideas such as light, travel, or life. Others stood for letters or sounds that could be combined to make words.

Chinese Word Symbols

THE CHINESE LANGUAGE is written with symbols (characters) that stand for sounds and words. The first-known Chinese writing dates to more than 1000 years after the invention of writing in Egypt and Mesopotamia. With few outside influences, these symbols changed little over the ages, making modern Chinese the oldest writing in use today. A dictionary from 1716 lists more than 40,000 characters. Each character was written with a brush, using 11 basic strokes. The painting of these beautiful characters is called calligraphy, and was always seen as a form of art.

Before the Chinese began using woodblocks for printing in 1600 B.C., books were often handwritten on bamboo strips. Movable type was invented in the A.D. 1040s. The Chinese also invented paper, nearly 2,000 years ago. Cloth or bark was shredded, pulped, and dried on frames. Ancient writings included poetry, practical handbooks, and encyclopedias. During the 1500s, popular folk tales such as *The Water Margin* were published, and about 200 years later, the writer Cao Xuequin produced the novel, *A Dream of Red Mansions.*

MAGICAL MESSAGES
The earliest surviving Chinese script appears on animal bones. They were used for telling fortunes in about 1200 B.C. The script was made up of small pictures representing objects or ideas. Modern Chinese script is made up of patterns of lines.

ART OF CALLIGRAPHY
This text was handwritten during the Tang dynasty (A.D. 618–906). Traditional Chinese writing reads down from right to left, starting in the top right-hand corner.

漢興六十餘載海
內艾安府庫充實
而四裔未賓制度
闕上方欲用文
武求之如弗及始
以蒲輪迎枚生見
主父偃徐樂嚴安
出於布衣各
慕義亦彬彬稍進
式擇於賢諸公孫
弘以儒雅顯董石
建石慶以篤行為
版築飯牛之朋亦
或降於斯已而
漢之得人於茲為
盛儒雅則公孫弘
董仲舒兒寬篤行
則石建石慶質直
則汲黯卜式推賢
則韓安國鄭當時
定令則趙禹張湯
文章則司馬遷相
如滑稽則東方朔
枚皋應對則嚴助
朱賈臣下
部各周惡
孝下臣意数劉
朱賈臣唐蒙喜助

MAKE PRINTING BLOCKS

You will need: plain white paper, pencil, paint, soft Chinese brush or thin paintbrush, water pot, tracing paper, board, self-drying clay (6 x 8 in., 1 in. thick), modeling tool, wood glue, block printing ink, damp rag.

1 Copy or trace the characters from the reversed image block (see opposite). Start off with a pencil outline, then fill in with paint. Let dry.

2 Copy design onto tracing paper. Turn the paper over. Place it on the clay. Scribble on the clean side of the paper to leave a mirror image in the clay.

3 Use a modeling tool to carve out characters. Cut away clay all around characters to make a relief (raised pattern). Smooth clay base with your fingertips.

THE BEST WAY TO WRITE

A calligrapher of the 1840s begins to write, surrounded by his assistants. The brush must be held upright for the writing of Chinese characters. The wrist is never rested on the table. Many years of practice and study are necessary to become a good calligrapher.

INKS AND COLORS

The watercolors and inks used for Chinese calligraphy were based on plant and mineral pigments in reds, blues, greens, and yellows. Black ink was made from carbon, obtained from soot. This was mixed with glue to form a solid block. The ink block was wetted during use. Brushes were made from animal hair fitted into bamboo handles.

Chinese brushes

THE PRINTED PAGE

The Buddhist scripture called the *Diamond Sutra (shown right)* is probably the oldest surviving printed book in the world. It includes both text and pictures. The book was printed from a wood block on May 11 A.D. 868 and was intended to be distributed to the public free of charge.

reversed image *actual image*

Block rubbings of characters were an early form of printing.

4 When the relief has dried, paint the clay block with wood glue. Let dry thoroughly. When dry, the glue seals and protects the pattern.

5 Now paint the design. Apply a thick layer of printing ink to the raised parts of the clay with a Chinese brush or a soft paintbrush.

6 Lay a thin piece of plain white paper over the inked block. Use a dry brush to press the paper into the ink, so that the paper takes up the design.

7 Lift up the paper to reveal your design. Take care of your printing block by cleaning it with a damp rag. You can then use it again and again.

Celtic Messages in Stone

IN EUROPE, the Celts had several different languages, but no single Celtic alphabet. To write something down, the Celts had to borrow other peoples' scripts. Sometimes they used Greek letters, sometimes Latin (the Romans' language). In the British Isles, a script known as Ogham was based on the Latin alphabet, but used straight lines instead of letters. Celtic craftworkers used all these different ways of writing to carve messages in stone. Their inscriptions might commemorate an important event, or a person who had died, or be a proud symbol of a leader's power. Craftworkers also decorated stones with beautiful patterns, sometimes copied from jewelry and metalworking designs. In some parts of Celtic Europe, standing stones and lumps of rock were carved with special symbols. Historians believe that these picture-carvings were designed to increase respect for powerful leaders, and for the gods.

STANDING STONE
Tall, carved standing stones were a special feature of Celtic lands in northwest France and Ireland. Archaeologists are not sure why they were put up or decorated, but they probably marked boundaries or holy sites. This stone comes from Turoe, in Ireland.

PRACTICE MAKES PERFECT
Before using precious metals such as gold, or starting to chip away at hard, valuable materials such as stone, craftworkers made sketches and worked out patterns on little pieces of bone. These bone fragments, marked with compass designs, were found in Ireland. They belonged to craftworkers from around A.D. 50.

MAKE AN OGHAM STONE

You will need: modeling clay, board, rolling pin, ruler, modeling tool, white paint, paintbrush, sandpaper, white glue, green cardboard, scissors.

1 Roll out the modeling clay to make a strip roughly 13 in. long, 2 in. wide and 1¼ in. thick. Carefully shape the top as shown.

2 Take the modeling tool and make a hole in the top end of the strip. This tall "holed" Ogham stone is based on one in southern Ireland from A.D. 400.

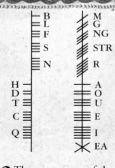

3 These are some of the Ogham letters.

ON LIVING ROCK

This rough slab of stone is decorated with a carving of a wild boar. It was found in Dunadd, Scotland. Archaeologists have many theories as to why it was carved. It may have been a memorial to a dead leader or a notice announcing an alliance between friendly clans. An alternative view is that it was a tribal symbol, put up as a proud boast of the local peoples' power or a sign of a local chieftain's land.

THE CELTS LIVE ON

The Picts were a mysterious people who lived in Scotland from about A.D. 300 to 900. They were descended from Celtic people and they continued many of the Celts' customs and traditions. In particular, they carved picture-symbols and Ogham letters on stone slabs, in caves and on lumps of rock. This stone monument, from Orkney, Scotland, shows three warriors and various other common Pictish symbols.

ALL CHANGE

Many tall, carved stones had religious power for the Celts. When Christian missionaries arrived in Celtic lands, they sometimes decided to make old carved stones into Christian monuments. They hoped this might help people understand that the Christian God was more important than the old Celtic ones. This stone is at Oronsay in the Orkney Islands off the northeast coast of Scotland.

Ogham is sometimes referred to as the "tree alphabet" because each letter takes the name of a tree. In many cases the Ogham inscription on a stone is read from the bottom up and contains the name of the person being commemorated and that of the carver.

4 Ogham writing is done as a series of lines or notches scored across a long stem. Use the alphabet in step 3 to help you write something on your stone.

5 Ogham inscriptions are often found on memorials featuring a person's name. You could try writing your name on your model Ogham stone.

6 Sand the modeling clay gently to remove any rough edges. Then paint one side of your stone. Let dry, turn over and paint the other side.

7 Cut a circular base out of green cardboard, roughly 5½ in. wide. Glue the bottom of your stone onto the base, as shown. Now let the stone dry.

Mesoamerican Writing

THE MAYA OF CENTRAL AMERICA were the first—and only—Mesoamerican people to invent a complete writing system. By A.D. 250, Maya picture symbols and sound symbols were written in books, carved on buildings, painted on pottery, and inscribed on precious stones. Maya scribes also developed an advanced number system, including a sign for zero, which Europeans at the time did not have.

Maya writing used glyphs (pictures standing for words) and also picture signs that stood for sounds. The sound signs could be joined together, like the letters of the Roman alphabet, to make words and complete sentences. The Aztecs used picture writing too, but theirs was much simpler and less flexible. Maya and Aztec picture symbols were difficult to learn. Only specially trained scribes could write them, and only priests or rich people could read them. They could spare time for study and afford to pay a good teacher.

MAYA READER
A Maya statue showing a wealthy woman seated cross-legged with a codex (folding book) on her lap. A Maya or Aztec codex was made of long strips of fig-bark paper, folded like a concertina. The writing was read from top to bottom and left to right.

CITY EMBLEM
Four separate images make up this emblem glyph for the Maya city-state of Copan. Together they give a message meaning "the home of the rulers of the royal blood of Copan." At the bottom, you can see a bat, the special picture sign for the city.

MAKE A CODEX

You will need: thin cardboard, ruler, pencil, scissors, white acrylic paint, eraser, large and small paintbrushes, water pot, paints in red, yellow, blue, and black, palette, tracing paper.

1 Draw a rectangle about 39½ x 10 in. onto thin cardboard. Cut the rectangle out. Cover it evenly with white acrylic paint. Let it dry.

2 Using a pencil and ruler, lightly draw in four fold-lines 8 in. apart. This will divide the painted cardboard into five equal sections.

3 Carefully fold along the pencil lines to make a zig-zag book, as shown. Unfold the cardboard and rub out the pencil lines with an eraser.

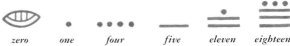

MAYA CODEX

Maya scribes wrote thousands of codices (folding, hand-painted books), but only four survive. All the rest were destroyed by Spanish missionaries. These pages from a Maya codex show the activities of several different gods. The figure at the top, painted black with a long nose, is Ek Chuah, the god of merchants.

| zero | one | four | five | eleven | eighteen |

AZTEC ENCYCLOPEDIA

These pictures of Aztec gods come from a book known as the Florentine Codex. This encyclopedia was compiled between 1547 and 1569 by Father Bernardino de Sahagun, a Spanish friar. He was fascinated by Aztec civilization and wanted to record it before it disappeared. This codex is the most complete written record of Aztec life we have.

MAYA NUMBERS

The Maya number system used only three signs—a dot for one, a bar for five, and the shell symbol for zero. Other numbers were made by using a combination of those signs. When writing down large numbers, Maya scribes put the different symbols on top of one another, rather than side by side as we do today.

4 Trace or copy Aztec or Maya codex drawings from this book. Alternatively, make up your own, based on Mesoamerican examples.

5 Paint your tracings or drawings, using light, bright colors. Using the Maya numbers on this page as a guide, add some numbers to your codex.

If you went to school in Aztec or Maya times, you would find out how to recognize hundreds of different picture symbols. You would also be taught to link them together in your mind, like a series of clues, to find out what they meant.

Glossary

A

alabaster A gleaming white stone, a type of gypsum.

amethyst A purple crystal, a type of quartz.

ancestor A family member who died long ago.

archaeology The scientific study of the past looking at the things people left behind, such as tools.

Arctic The region in the far north of our planet, surrounding the North Pole.

auloi A pair of musical pipes used in ancient Greece. One pipe produced the melody while the other produced a background drone.

Aztecs Mesoamerican people who lived in nothern and central Mexico.

B

bards In Celtic times, bards were well-educated poets. Becoming a bard was the first step in the long process of becoming a druid.

booty Valuable things taken away by a victorious army.

bronze A metal made by mixing tin with copper.

burial ship Finely decorated ships in which Vikings were sometimes buried or cremated.

C

civilization A society that has made advances in arts, science and technology, law, or government.

collyrium A black paste used as an eyeliner.

courtier A person attending at royal court.

D

dhoti Traditional Indian dress worn by Hindu men.

druid Celtic priests. According to Roman writers, there were three stages to becoming a druid. Some studied the natural world and claimed to foresee the future. Some were bards that knew about history. Some led Celtic worship, made sacrifices to the gods, and administered holy laws.

dynasty A period of rule by emperors of the same royal family.

E

emperor The ruler of a group of lands known as an empire.

F

faience A type of opaque glass that is often blue or green. It is made from quartz or sand, lime, ash and natron.

feud A long-standing quarrel, especially between two families.

G

geometry A branch of mathematics concerning the measurements of lines, angles and surfaces. It was pioneered by the Greek scientist Euclid. In Greek, it means measuring the land.

gladiator A professional fighter in Roman times, a slave, or a criminal who fought to the death for public entertainment.

gorgon A female monster of such horrific appearance that anyone who looked at her died.

H

henna A reddish dye for the hair or skin, made from the leaves of a shrub.

Hinduism Religion that includes the worship of several gods and belief in reincarnation.

I

imperial Relating to the rule of an emperor or empress.

inro A small, decorated box, worn hanging from the belt in Japan.

Inuit An ancient people of the Arctic. The name simply means "the people."

Islam Religion of Muslim people.

ivory The hard, smooth, cream-colored part of the tusks of elephants and walruses.

K

kabuki Popular plays, performed in Japan from about A.D. 1600. They were fast moving and loud.

kaolin A fine white clay used in porcelain and paper making.

kimono A loose robe with wide sleeves worn by Japanese men and women.

L

lacquer A thick, colored varnish, used to coat wood, metal, or leather.

lapis lazuli A dark blue, semi-precious stone used for jewelry.

llama A camel-like creature of South America.

lyre One of the various harp-like instruments played in ancient Greece and Rome.

M

mammals A type of warm-blooded animal such as human beings, whales, bats, and cats.

martial arts Physical exercises that are often based on combat, such as sword play and kung fu. Chinese martial arts bring together spiritual and physical disciplines.

Mesoamerica Central America.

minotaur A mythical beast, half man, half bull, that lived in a maze under a palace in Crete. It was slain by the Greek hero, Theseus.

mosaics A picture or decorated object made up of many small squares or cubes of glass, stone or pottery, set in soft concrete.

mother-of-pearl A hard, shiny substance found in shells, also known as nacre. It was often used in inlays by skilled Chinese craftsman.

myth An ancient story of gods and heroes.

N

netsuke Small toggles, carved from ivory and used to attach items to belts in Japan.

nobles People who are high in social rank.

noh A serious, dignified drama that originated in Japan around 1300.

Norman A descendant of the Vikings in Europe, who settled in northern France.

O

obi A wide sash, worn only by women in Japan.

ocher A yellow—or red-colored earth used as pigment in paint.

Odin The most powerful and mysterious Viking God. He was the god of war, magic, and poetry.

Olmec A Mesoamerican people who lived in southern central Mexico. Their civilization existed between 1200 B.C. and 400 B.C.

Olympic Games A sporting competition held every year at Olympia in ancient Greece in honor of the god Zeus. The first games were held in 776 B.C.

P

papyrus A tall, reedy plant that grows on the River Nile in Egypt. It was used for making paper.

peske Thick fur parka worn by Saami people in the Arctic over their tunics.

pharaoh Ruler of ancient Egypt.

pigment Any material used to provide color for paint or ink.

porcelain The finest quality of pottery. It was made from kaolin and baked at a high temperature.

pyxis A box used for storing face powder or other cosmetics in Greece.

R

ritual An often repeated set of actions carried out during a religious ceremony.

S

sari Traditional dress for women in India.

shamisen A traditional Japanese three-stringed musical instrument.

shogun A Japanese army commander. From 1185–1868, shoguns ruled Japan.

smelt To extract a metal from its ore by heating it in a furnace.

sphinx A creature with a lion's head and a human's body.

surcoat A long, loose tunic worn over armor in Japan.

T

tapestry A cloth with a picture or design woven by hand on its threads.

terra-cotta Baked, unglazed, orange-red clay.

Thor The fierce Viking god of thunder.

timpanon A tambourine made with animal skin.

tipi Conical tent with a frame of poles, covered with animal skins, used by Plains Indians.

totem pole A tall post carved with good luck charms.

tribe A group of people who share a common language and way of life.

turban Headdress worn by Sikh, Muslim, and some Hindu men.

V

Viking One of the Scandinavian peoples who lived by sea-raiding in the early Middle Ages.

W

walrus A sea mammal with long tusks.

X

xiang qi A traditional Chinese board game, similar to that of chess.

Index